TOO BLESSED

To Be

CURSED

**Deliverance from Curses
through the Power of the Blood of
Jesus Christ**

Kenneth Scott

Scriptures in this publication are taken from the King James version of the Bible or paraphrased by the author.

Too Blessed to be Cursed

P10

Deliverance from Curses Through the Power of the Blood of Jesus Christ

Table of Contents

Introduction

There are many curses in the Bible. The Following are a few of the kind of curses that you will find in the Bible.

- There are curses for gross sins and unrighteousness
- There are curses for disobeying God and failing to uphold His Word
- There are curses for hurting people and doing them wrong
- There are curses for dishonesty and unfairness in how you treat your brother
- There are curses for not keeping your word
- There are generational curses and sin curses

These and other curses are written throughout the Bible. Some of them only apply to the person who did the offense; in certain cases, the curses travel down the bloodline and is applied to another person in that family or generation. These things happened; they are in the Bible, and they are true. So then, how do we keep them from coming upon our lives and coming upon us and our descendents?

Come now therefore, I pray thee, curse me this
people; for they are too mighty for me: perad-
venture I shall prevail, that we may smite
them, and that I may drive them out of the
land: for I [know] that he whom thou blessest
is blessed, and he whom thou cursest is
cursed. (Num 22:6)

This passage is taken from the story of Balaam and
Balak. Balaam was an Old Testament wicked prophet
for hire. King Balak feared the Israelites and tried to get
Balaam to curse them rather than attempt to fight them.
King Balak had heard of the victories that God had given
the Israelites and knew they could not defeat them in
battle. Instead, he attempted to defeat them by hiring
Balaam to curse them.

How can I curse those whom God has not cursed? *How can I denounce those whom the LORD has not denounced? (Num 23:8 NIV)*

It is apparent that Balaam previously had much
success in cursing and blessing people. He was well
known for using his trade and gift for hire. He was so
known that even the king sought to hire him. It seemed
that in the past, whomever Balaam put a curse on was
cursed, and whomever he blessed would receive a blessing.

Can't Touch This

When Balaam was summoned by King Balak to put
a curse on the Israelites, even though Balaam was
offered a king's reward to curse them, he could not do it.
Every time Balak took him to a place to curse the Israel-

ites, he would end up uttering blessings out of his mouth instead. Balak took him to several places to curse the Israelites, but the same thing kept happening.

Even through Balaam was successful in cursing others in the past, he could not curse the Israelites at all no matter how much money he was offered.

The reason why he could not curse them is because they were covered by God. They had God with them; He was among them, covering them, and protecting them. There is nothing in God that can be cursed, and neither can anything around God be cursed. And, as Rom 8:31 says, *if God is for us (or with us), then nothing is strong enough, powerful enough, or able to stand against us and succeed.* So although Balaam was successful in cursing many other people, he could not touch the people of God.

It's the same with us today. The curses that are in the Bible are just as real today as they were thousands of years ago. Those who are not born-again, not covered by the blood of Jesus Christ, and do not confess and stand on the power and protection of the blood of Jesus Christ, they and their family line are still very much vulnerable and susceptible to these curses.

These curses can be very bad and can go on for decades. But those who are born-again and properly covered by the Blood of Jesus, and exercise their faith through praying, speaking, and confessing the Word of God are exempt from these curses in the same way that the Children of Israel were exempt from Balaam's curses. The difference is the sacrifice of the cross and the blood of Jesus Christ over our lives. THAT'S THE DIFFERENCE!

In all Thy Getting, Get Understanding

Proverbs 4:7 tells us *that in all thy getting, to get an understanding.* It is imperative that you read this entire book so that you will be able to get the full understanding of what is being taught about curses and generational curses. Don't just quote the scriptures and confessions at the end of the book. After reading the complete book you will find out how and why God allowed curses upon man in the first place, and you will find the different ways curses came upon man. But most importantly, you will come to understand how to appropriate the power of the blood of Jesus to your life and family lives that exempts you and your family from these curses.

So get ready to learn the truth about curses and generational curses. And, get ready to walk in the power of God and begin breaking curses from your life, your family lives, and the lives of others.

Chapter 1

Do Generational Curses Still Exist?

Think not that I am come to destroy the law, or the prophets: I am not come to destroy, but to fulfil. (Matthew 5:17)

In this passage, when Jesus said that He did not come to destroy "*the law,*" the "*law*" He is referring to is the Old Testament law. Jesus is saying that He did not come to do away with the Old Testament law, but rather, "*to fulfill*" the law. This means that He came to reveal and uncover the true spiritual meaning of the law as it relates to Him.

The entire Bible is a book about Christ. There are some who think that only the New Testament is about Christ. This is not true at all. In every book of the Bible from Genesis to Revelation is the story of how Satan deceived us and lured us into sin, and as a result, we were lost, defeated, and destined for the eternal wrath of God. But every book of the Bible also entails how Christ came to save us, redeem us, deliver us, and restore us back to God's favor, blessings, and His physical as well as His eternal salvation.

11

The Old Testament showed this in the physical lives and journeys of the Israelites. The New Testament shows this in the life, works, Words, and revelation of Jesus Christ. The Old Testament shows Christ concealed. The New Testament shows Christ revealed.

For Example: Under the old covenant law we needed a priest to go before us to make sacrifices unto the Lord. Under the new law we no longer need a priest to represent us and make sacrifices for us. Jesus Christ is now our High Priest who sits on the right hand of the Father making intercession for us.

Under the old law, animal sacrifices were required to atone for our sins. Under the new covenant, we no longer have to make animal sacrifices. Jesus became the final sacrificial lamb for all the sins of all mankind. Under the old law, they had to keep the Sabbath day or suffer the wrath of God for their disobedience. Under the new covenant we understand that when Christ died, He became our Sabbath (our place of rest). The Sabbath is no longer a day, but rather, the person, the rest, and the finished work of Jesus Christ. Under the old covenant, all the young men had to be circumcised on the eighth day. Any male who was not circumcised was considered an enemy of God. In addition, anyone living in the house of an uncircumcised male was also considered an enemy of God. Under the new covenant, the physical circumcision is no longer necessary. Circumcision is now a spiritual act, which is a cutting away of the flesh. Spiritual circumcision is the cutting away of the sinful lusts, cravings, and deeds of the flesh.

As you can see with these examples, none of these laws were abolished. There is not one Old Testament law in the entire Bible that was abolished. Jesus came to show us the real, true, spiritual meaning and reason for the law as it relates to Him. God still holds us accountable to each and every one of His laws. The difference is that many of them are now fulfilled through Christ, His blood, His sufferings, and His sacrifice on the cross.

The law of curses and generational curses are no different. They still exist. But for those who are in Christ and who implement the power of the Word of God and blood of Jesus Christ into their lives, the curses have no effect on us.

Chapter 2

The Famine

We will now look into the life of David and find where David and the Israelites experienced a generational curse. We will also see what they did and how God gave them the answer and deliverance.

Then there was a famine in the days of David three years, year after year...(2 Samuel 21:1)

David and the Israelites experienced a famine for three years in a row. A famine is a time when nothing grows upon the land. As a result of nothing growing, animals die, and the people go hungry and even starve. As we will discover, David and the Israelites experienced this famine because of a generational curse.

We can also experience spiritual famines because of generational curses. A spiritual famine is when nothing seems to grow, increase, or progress in our lives or families in a particular area. We can experience a famine in our health where we are hit with sickness and disease and do not receive our healing. We can experience a famine in our finances where it seems we just continue to struggle financially over and over again. And we can also experience famines in our jobs, where we cannot seem to find a job, keep a job, or get a promotion on our job. These are just a few of the different types of famines that can hit us. They can literally hit us in any area of our lives.

The Covenant with the Gibeonites

Then there was a famine in the days of David three years, year after year; and David inquired of the LORD. And the LORD answered, it is for Saul, and for his bloody house, because he slew <u>*the Gibeonites.*</u> *(2 Samuel 21:1)*

After David tried everything in his power to avert the famine, he finally decided to seek the face of the Lord for the answer as to why he was having this recurring problem. As he sought the Lord, God then gave David the reason for this curse. It was because of what Saul had done to the Gibeonites. But in order to understand the significance of God's answer to David, I need to go back and give you a little historical background on what happened with the Gibeonites.

The book of Joshua begins with the account of the children of Israel's invasion of the Promised Land under Joshua's regime. This took place 40 years after Moses' generation failed to take the land because of their sins, lack of faith, and their fear. God told Joshua and the Israelites to go over and take everything. After they had successfully taken Jericho and the next city of Ai, they were on their way to their third conquest, which was supposed to be the city of Gibeon. But the people of Gibeon had heard of the great and mighty exploits of God through the Israelites. They had heard of the miracles in Egypt, and how God delivered them from Pharaoh and Egypt (the world power of that time). They heard how God had parted the Red Sea and brought them across on dry land. They heard how He had provided for them for forty years in the desert wilderness. They had also heard about the miraculous miracle at Jericho, and their victory over the capital city of Ai.

They knew that there was no possible way they could defeat this nation with God behind them, so they resorted to trickery. They sent ambassadors to intercept Joshua and the Israelites about a three day's journey before they would have reached Gibeon. They deceptively disguised these ambassadors to look as though they had been traveling for months. They had molded bread, wineskins that were busted and worn, shoes that had holes in them, and their clothes were worn and torn.

The ambassadors told Joshua that they were from a distant continent, and had been traveling for months. They also told Joshua that they had heard about the greatness of their God, and wanted to make a covenant with them to serve their God. They asked Joshua and the Israelites to make a covenant with them; they also promised that with this covenant, they would both serve them and pay them taxes.

Since Joshua was under the supposition they were not part of the Promised Land, they considered this proposal from the Gibeonites to be an unexpected extra blessing. So without seeking God, they went ahead and made the covenant with them and continued on their way.

After a three day's journey to their next conquest, they ran into the Gibeonites. Even though they tricked Joshua and the Israelites into making the covenant with them, it was still a binding covenant because they made the covenant in the presence and witness of God. Part of the Israelites covenant with them was that they promised not to kill or harm them. Because of this covenant promise, they were allowed to live, but Joshua made them servants, made them pay taxes, and tasked them with hard work among them in the land. The Gibeonites therefore lived among them and served them.

Saul Destroys the Gibeonites

...And David inquired of the LORD. And the LORD answered, <u>it is for Saul, and for his bloody house, because he slew the Gibeonites</u>. (*2 Samuel 21:1*)

Generations later, Saul becomes king. By this time, the Gibeonites had been living among the Israelites for many years. They served them and paid the Israelites taxes. One day while Saul was in one of his rages, he decided that the Gibeonites should not be allowed to live among them, and went on a rampage killing hundreds of them. This became a great sin because of the covenant that Joshua and the Israelites had made before God with the Gibeonites several generations earlier not to harm them.

A generation after this, Saul is now dead and David becomes the king. At that time David was living comfortably in his new position with all going well for him in the kingdom. Then all of a sudden a devastating famine broke out three years in a row. After David had done everything he knew to do, he finally sought the Lord as to the cause of the famine after the third year. God revealed to David that this famine was a curse that was placed upon the Israelites because of the sins of Saul a generation earlier. Even though Saul was now dead, God was judging the Israelites for something that Saul's generation had done.

The Substitute Judgment

*And they answered the king, The man that con-
sumed us, and that devised against us that we
should be destroyed from remaining in any of the
coasts of Israel, let seven men of his sons be delivered unto us, and we will hang them up unto the
LORD in Gibeah of Saul, whom the LORD did
choose. And the king said, I will give them. (2
Samuel 21:5-6)*

After God revealed to David that they were under a
generational curse because of what Saul had done to the
Gibeonites, David went to inquire of them of what they
wanted in order to get released from the curse. The
Gibeonites' answer to David was that they wanted him to
give them seven sons of Saul to hang for the revenge of Saul
ordering the slaughter of so many of their people.

To understand the Bible, especially the Old Testament,
you must first understand the "Law of Representation." In
this Law of Representation, the Gibeonites were the ones
who were offended. This offense took place in a previous
generation. Just because the penalty was not carried out
upon Saul during his lifetime does not mean that the trespass or offense must go unpunished. After Saul's death, the
penalty became the responsibility of his descendants to
pay. Therefore, the Gibeonites represent the spirit of injustice that calls out to God for justice and vengeance for gross
wrongs and injustice that have gone unpunished and unpaid. When they asked for seven sons of Saul to be hung,
this represents the spirit of the Gibeonites rising up and
crying out to God for vengeance for the injustice done to
them even long after that person is dead and gone.

...the voice of thy brother's blood crieth unto me from the ground. And now art thou cursed from the earth... When thou tillest the ground, it shall not henceforth yield unto thee her strength... (Gen 4:10)

In many instances in the Bible, you find God telling a person that someone's blood was crying out to Him from the grave (Example Gen 4:10). This cry that God refers to in His Word is the spirit of the Gibeonites that cries from the grave when a person has done extreme evil to a person or group of people, and the penalty was not paid by the culprit during their natural, physical life. It's a constant cry for justice, vengeance and judgment. The spirit of the Gibeonites also cries out for other gross types of sin and unrighteousness that goes unpunished and unjudged during the person's earthly, physical life. Again, even though the person who committed the sins or transgressions may be dead and long gone, the penalty still can be paid. It's paid by the (sons) descendants.

Although King Saul began as a good king, he changed and disobeyed God and turned into an evil, unrighteous king. Saul was not judged physically during his lifetime for this evil act of murdering many of the Gibeonites; therefore, when the Gibeonites had a chance to ask for vengeance, they demanded the next best thing—seven of his sons. These seven sons of Saul became a "substitute" for Saul.

The sons of Saul, therefore, represent the *"Substitute Judgment."* The "Substitute Judgment" means that the person or people who committed a crime, transgression, or offense are not alive, so the spirit of the Gibeonites cries out from the grave to God for a relative substitute to take their place. This is what happened with the case of David and the Israelites. Since Saul was now dead, seven of his sons were requested for a comparable, relative substitute.

The same thing can hold true to our day. If a person committed a gross sin of offense against someone and they did not sincerely and correctly repent of that offense, or it was not effectively judged during their lifetime, the spirit of the Gibeonites can still come up to cry out to God for vengeance.

The Law of Inherited Debt

An example of substitute judgment can be found in the story of the widow woman and the pot of oil in 2 Kings Chapter 4. This widow woman's husband was a servant of God who served faithfully but was now dead. But in those days, if someone died owing money to a creditor, the children then became responsible for paying the debt. If they couldn't pay the debt, the creditor would have the right to either put them in jail, or make them their servants until the debt was paid.

In this story, the father died still owing the creditors. Neither the wife nor children had anything to pay the creditors. The creditors were now on their way to put the woman's two sons in jail and make them slaves until the debt was paid off. Even though they had nothing to do with making the loan, the children were still responsible for paying it off because the creditors could legally make the children responsible for paying the remainder of the loan.

God used Elisha to perform the miracle of the oil. The woman only had one pot of oil, but God multiplied the oil over and over again—filling up every vessel in her entire house with oil. She then went into the oil business and sold the oil, making enough money to pay the creditors off and still live off the rest, thus keeping her sons from being put in jail or servitude.

In this story, the reason the creditors could make the children responsible for the debt of their deceased father was because of the law of "Inherited Debt." This is a law that no longer exists in our society. In our society, once a person dies, the only thing that a creditor can make a stake or claim to is the property and assets that were owned by the deceased.

In the law of inherited debt that existed in those days, just as children could inherit property and assets from their deceased parents, they also inherited the responsibility of their deceased parents' debt. And, if they were unable to pay their creditors, they could be placed in jail or placed into servitude until the debt was fully paid.

Even though we no longer have the law of inherited debt in our society, it still exists spiritually. Generational curses operate under this form of substitute judgment with the law of inherited debt. Just as the sons of this widow woman inherited the debt responsibility of their father (even though he was dead), spiritually, we can also inherit (unpaid) debts of our ancestors. Generational curses serve as the payment for sin debts or gross offense against a person or group of people.

Before you become discouraged or troubled with this information, you will come to understand in our next two chapters how Jesus made a way of escape for us. He paid the debt for us and thereby removed the curse from mankind, setting us free from the curse and generational curses.

Chapter 3

The Curse in the Beginning

* **Note**: *In this chapter, the reference that is made to Adam most of the time is a reference to both Adam and Eve.*

In our first chapter, we have learned about curses, generational curses, famines, the physical Gibeonites, the spiritual Gibeonites, and what they represent. In this chapter, we want to look at how and why curses and generational curses came into the world and upon mankind, and how Christ has redeemed us from them and set us free.

In the Garden

When man was placed in the Garden of Eden, he had heavenly bliss. He had true heaven on earth. He had everything he wanted and needed. Adam enjoyed constant peace, internal rest and security, and unspeakable joy in his soul. Because of this divine connection, Adam did not have any worries, and lacked for nothing spiritually, physically, emotionally, or in any other means. He walked in God's divine authority and power. And best of all, he enjoyed full unencumbered fellowship and communion with God.

Adam enjoyed all these things until Satan lured him into sin. Adam then lost it all and was cast out of the garden. But not only did he lose everything, his disobedience and rebellion to God's Word also brought upon him (and mankind) a number of curses. But thanks be to God, who sent another Adam—the last Adam, who succeeded where the first Adam failed, and restored everything the first Adam lost.

The following passage is taken from Genesis where the curses for mankind were pronounced after the fall of the first Adam. But in addition, afterwards, it will show how the last Adam—Jesus Christ restored for us what the first Adam lost through the fall and curse.

The Curse of Adam and Mankind

The following scripture passage entails several parts of the curse that Adam brought on mankind. Let us look at these curses, and at the blessings of how Christ redeemed us from the curse of the fall.

> *And unto Adam he said, because thou hast hearkened unto the voice of thy wife, and hast eaten of the tree, of which I commanded thee, saying, Thou shalt not eat of it:* **_cursed is the ground for thy sake_**; *in sorrow shalt thou eat of it all the days of thy life; Thorns also and thistles shall it bring forth to thee; and thou shalt eat the herb of the field; In the sweat of thy face shalt thou eat bread, till thou return unto the ground; for out of it wast thou taken: for dust thou art, and unto dust shalt thou return. (Gen 3:17-19)*

...cursed is the ground for thy sake...

The Curse: God told Adam that because of his disobedience the ground would be cursed. When God created man, He created man from the dust of the ground. When God told Adam that the ground would be cursed, God was also telling Adam that mankind (which is made from the dust of the ground) would now be under a curse because of their sin and rebellion against His Word.

This portion of the curse refers to the ultimate curse—hell. In Romans 6:23 the Bible declares that the wages (curse of) sin is death. This death is a two-fold curse. First, it represents a separation from God. Because of the curse, man became separated from God. For thousands of years, man did not have direct communion with God. He had to go through a priest with the sacrificial blood of animals. This type of death lasted until Christ could come and become the final sacrificial lamb for all eternity. After Christ died, the veil in the temple was torn, signifying that there was no longer a separation from God, and that all who sought after God could have fellowship with Him.

The second part of this death-curse refers to the eternal separation from God. It is one thing to be separated from God for a season, but it's another thing to be separated from God for all eternity. This second death also represents the ultimate curse—hell. Hell was not prepared for mankind; it was prepared for Satan and his followers. But when man sinned and rebelled against God's Word, he automatically aligned with Satan, and therefore with the penalty that was set and established for Satan and his followers *(Matt 25:41)*.

Redemption: The bad news for mankind is that the wages

(curse) of sin is death. But thank God that He didn't stop there. He sent Jesus Christ to fulfill the latter part of this passage, which says, *but the gift of God is eternal life through Jesus Christ our Lord*. Satan thought he had defeated us. Satan knew that he was destined for eternal hell and punishment because of his rebellion. He also knew that God loved man and did not want to destroy man in hell. Satan thought that if he lured man into sin that he had God over a barrel—thinking that God would not destroy him because God did not want to destroy man. But thanks be to God for His wisdom, mercy, and love. God devised a plan in which He could punish Satan and his followers, punish sin, and yet save and redeem man. But this plan came at an extreme price—the life and suffering of His only Son. God punished the sin of man by putting all the sin of mankind upon His Son—Jesus Christ. This is why Jesus' sufferings were so extreme; He had to pay for the sins of mankind. Through Christ, God punished sin, redeemed man, and still reserved the eternal punishment of hell for Satan and his followers. But praise be to the Almighty God for the gift of eternal life through our Lord and Savior, Jesus Christ.

...In sorrow shalt thou eat of it all the days of thy life...

The Curse: Eating of sorrow was referring to the sorrow that would befall man. Many people attempt to blame God for the catastrophes, evils of men, diseases, and afflictions that we all see, hear and live through today in our world around us. But it's not God who brings them, nor is it God's fault they are here. Blaming God would be like a person speeding after seeing the posted speed limit and blaming the city or municipality for receiving a ticket. We can no more blame God for the evils of our day than the person who gets the ticket for speeding. The speeding ticket came because the person knowingly disobeyed and violated the law. All of the sorrows that mankind has lived through has been part of the original curse that was placed upon Adam and mankind because of sin and disobedience.

Redemption: The sorrows of this world are real, but they are only temporary. First of all, Jesus suffered and died on the cross to give us peace in our sorrows. He has given us the peace, comfort and strength of the Holy Spirit to take us through our sorrows. Secondly, because of Christ, our sorrows are now only temporary. Romans 8:18 declares that the sorrows of this world cannot even begin to compare to the blessings and glory that God has prepared for His people. It has been said that the sorrows of this world are like a drop of water compared to the waters of the ocean, to the glory and blessings that God has prepared for us. *...Eye hath not seen, nor ear heard, neither have entered into the heart of man, the things which God hath prepared for them that love him (1 Cor 2:9).*

...Thorns also and thistles shall it bring forth to thee...

The Curse: When thorns and thistles are in the ground, they choke and prohibit good plants and fruit from growing—leaving the ground dry and bare. It takes a lot of hard labor and work to transform a dry ground full of thorns and thistles and make it fertile. But God is saying here that even with your hard work and efforts, the ground is only going to bring more thorns and thistles.

Thorns and thistles represent evil and wicked things

that come to destroy the good that we desire and hope for. This is exactly what a curse does. It destroys the goodness and good things of life. Curses that are upon the land cause the land to produce a famine, whereby no food or nourishment can grow from it. A curse does the same thing. It hinders growth, prosperity, blessings, and goodness that were originally intended for us. This curse represented that no matter how hard man attempted to work to obtain the good of man, thorns and thistles would continue to grow up.

Redemption: In John 10:10, Jesus said that He came to give us life and life more abundantly. Jesus was not merely just talking about heaven; He was also talking about this life here on earth. Through Christ, we can reverse the curse of famines and destruction in our lives and family. For every act of stealing, killing, and destruction that the enemy attempts to bring upon our lives, through Christ, we can decree, declare and receive His abundant life even while we are here on earth. The abundant life of Christ is not limited to material things. The abundant life of Christ also consists of righteousness, peace, and joy in the Holy Ghost.

..And thou shalt eat the herb of the field...

The Curse: Eating bitter herbs represent receiving sufferings and hardship. They also represent war and destruction. Man has been attempting to obtain peace and tranquility on earth since the beginning. But instead, we have had continued war, calamity, and destruction. Even though there are many who have a chance to enjoy seasons of peace and prosperity, humanity as a whole have never enjoyed sustained, long-lasting peace because of the curse of bitter herbs that was given to man as a result of man's sin and rebellion.

Redemption: In Isaiah 53:5 the Bible declares that the chastisement of our peace was laid upon Him (Christ). God is pure holiness, goodness, godliness, and righteousness. Because of this, when sin entered the soul of man, man was automatically set at war with God. There was no peace and unity in the spirit and soul of man with the spirit of God. But Jesus ate the bitter herbs of the sufferings on the cross for us. Through the bitter herbs that He ate, He ended the war of the sinful and rebellious soul of man with the holiness and righteousness of God. The blood of Jesus Christ has covered and cleansed our soul of sins, iniquities, and transgressions. As a result, His blood has made peace with man and God. We can now come boldly before the throne of God in prayer and have intimate fellowship with God. Praise God! The war is over!

...In the sweat of thy face shalt thou eat bread...

The Curse: The "sweat" in this passage had a double-fold meaning. First, it represented Adam losing his god-like authority. Remember we said earlier that Adam did not physically work. He spoke things into existence because God made him as a speaking spirit. So this part of this curse represented Adam losing his speaking spirit authority.

Redemption: Adam did lose his speaking spirit authority. But through Christ, God has given it back to us. Christ has given us the power and authority to speak His Word. When we now speak the Word of God, we are not simply speaking vain and empty words. They are words of God's power and authority. Through speaking and confessing the Word of God, we can now change our lives, circumstances, and surroundings. We can now form our lives and world around us by the Word (of God) we speak.

The Sweat of Hard Work

The second meaning of Adam having to sweat refers to hard work. Adam now had to physically labor and work hard to obtain that which he once easily received. In the beginning, Adam's spirit was right and in tune with God, and Adam pleased God and enjoyed daily fellowship and commune with Him. Because of the curse, the only way Adam could now please God was through the hard work of attempting to keep the law. The problem is that even though God's laws are pure and perfect, the law is very hard and difficult to completely follow and obey. All of man's hard work and self-efforts to please God through obeying the law has failed miserably.

Redemption: Even though Adam and mankind failed miserably in an attempt to please God by keeping the law, the last Adam succeeded. Jesus Christ came into this world as a man and fully complied with, obeyed, and followed every one of the laws, statutes, ordinances, and precepts of God. He therefore fully and completely pleased God. God declared to the whole World that *Jesus Christ is His beloved Son in whom He is well pleased.*
Now, through Christ, instead of trying to please God only through the hard work of our futile self-efforts to keep and obey the law, we please God when we become born-again

and receive Christ into our hearts and lives. We also please Him whenever we come before Him in the name, Spirit, and Word of God. When we become born-again, we put on Christ, we put on His fragrance, we put on His presence, and we put on His Spirit. Christ is now our covering! Christ is now our righteousness! And, through Christ we now please God.

...till thou return unto the ground; for out of it wast thou taken: for dust thou art, and unto dust shalt thou return.

The Curse: Returning to the ground represents physical death. God did not originally make man to get sick, grow old, or to die. Man was originally made to live forever in a perfect condition. But man's sin and rebellion to God's Word brought sickness, disease, old age, and death (returning to the ground) upon all mankind.

Redemption: The wonderful blessing is that because of Christ we won't have to stay in the ground. The ground is only where our bodies will return. Christ died and was buried, but He was the firstborn that was raised from the dead to live for eternity. Because of Christ, our soul will not remain in the dust of the grave. It will be raised by Christ, through Christ, and to live with Christ, forever!

The Contrast Between the Two Gardens

We began this chapter by showing the fall of Adam and the curse that was pronounced on Adam and mankind because of the fall. We also showed the contrast of how the last Adam redeemed us and restored that in which the first

Adam failed and lost. Even though the first Adam lost everything in the beginning in the Garden of Eden, there was another garden (the Garden of Gethsemane) that was the beginning of the restoration of everything that the first Adam lost.

And being in agony he prayed more earnestly: and his sweat was as it were great drops of blood falling down to the ground. (Luke 22:44)

The first blood that was shed by Jesus was not shed on the cross; it was shed in the Garden of Gethsemane. Our salvation, authority, and perfect commune with God were all lost in the Garden of Eden through Adam's disobedience. However, our victory, restoration, and redemption were won and restored to us through Jesus' sweat and blood in the Garden of Gethsemane.

Because of Adam's disobedience, the curse of sweat was pronounced upon Adam and mankind. But thank God that Jesus sweat for us. While He was toiling in prayer, He was under such agony and anguish that He sweat while He was in prayer. But the sweat of Christ was not just simply sweat; it was mingled with His blood. The blood that Jesus sweat washed away Adam's sweat (the curse that came upon mankind because of sin and disobedience) and freed us from the original curse, generational curses, and every curse of men and of demons and devils. Thank God that Jesus sweat blood for us. Because of His blood-sweat, we are now set free!

Chapter 4

The Thorns and the Cross

The Crown of Thorns

In our previous chapter we showed how the curse came upon Adam and mankind in the beginning (in the book of Genesis) as a result of sin, rebellion, and disobedience. We also showed how Jesus (who is called the last Adam) came to redeem us, set us free, and break the curses that were pronounced upon mankind because of man's disobedience. Now that we have discovered how Christ has delivered us from curses and generational curses, let us look closer at two specific things in which Christ used to deliver us. First, let us look at the crown of thorns.

*And the soldiers twisted a **crown of thorns** and put it on His head, and they put on Him a purple robe. (John 19:2)*

After Jesus had endured a relentless tortuous flogging, the Roman soldiers twisted together a crown of thorns into

33

a circle, placed it on Jesus' head, and mashed it into His scalp. Anyone who has been caught in a thorn bush or has been pricked or scratched by them knows that they can be very painful. In addition, the types of thorns that grow in the Middle East are much harder and larger than those that grow in the west. For them to somehow twist them in a circle and mash them into His scalp must have been brutally painful and bloody.

Through this mockery and public humiliation, the Roman soldiers were attempting to make a laughingstock and a spectacle of Jesus, while attempting to poke fun and humor of the charges that were made against Him—of being King of the Jews. But what they meant as mockery and a joke became a prophetic example and demonstration of who Christ was, who He is, what He has done, and who He has become.

The Crown – a Symbol of Christ's Lordship

First, the crown of thorns represents Jesus as our eternal King. The scripture tells us that *every knee shall bow and every tongue shall confess that Jesus Christ is Lord.* He is the King of all kings and the Lord of all lords. He was the suffering servant, but yet He has now become the conquering King (Isaiah 53 and Revelations 19).

He conquered Satan, sin, and all temptations. He endured the pain and sufferings to redeem us. Now, instead of a crown of thorns, He has received the crown of all glory and honor. And, He is seated on the throne of majesty, in the highest place in all the heavens and the universe—at the right hand of God the Father Almighty.

The Crown—Redemption from the Curse

But that which beareth <u>thorns and briers</u> is rejected, and is nigh unto <u>cursing</u>... (Heb 6:8)

The second thing the crown of thorns represents is the curse. In the above passage, it refers to a curse being given to the one who wears thorns and briers. This was a prophetic Word referring to Jesus Christ—the one who wore the crown of thorns and took away our curses.

Now, let us look back at the curse of thorns that was prophesied in Genesis. In our previous chapter, we saw how God declared the curse of the thorns upon Adam and mankind because of sin. We said that thorns and thistles represent the curse of famine, destruction, and hindrance. An example of this type of curse would be the famine (curse) that David and the Israelites experienced.

It's a redundant, reoccurring, recycling curse that continues—person after person, family after family, or generation after generation. This curse stops the flow of blessings in our lives. It can cause famines and hindrances in our finances, health, emotional well-being, relationships (marriage and family) and any other area. Until this curse is fully paid or redeemed, it is passed down from family to family and from generation to generation.

The Buck Stops Here!

Thanks God for Jesus Christ, our redeemer, who didn't leave us with the curse of the thorns upon mankind. Jesus wore the crown of thorns on His head to show that He has put an end to the curse of the thorns and thistles.

President Truman made a well-known phrase popular

with a sign that he portrayed on his desk. The sign read, *"The Buck Stops Here."* It was a response to a slang which is still popular and used today, that says, *"Pass the Buck."* This is a slang that refers to passing responsibility and blame to someone else and continuing to pass it on and on. Politicians are experts in operating in this slang. By Jesus wearing the crown of thorns on His head, He was in essence wearing a sign that made a declaration to humanity and to every demon and demonic spirit that, ***"The Curse Stops HERE!"***

When someone is anointed in the Bible, they are usually anointed upon the head. When oil is poured on someone it is usually poured and flows from the head down. This is done because the head represents the whole body. When you lay hands upon someone's head and pray for them, you are in essence laying hands upon and praying for their entire body.

When curses (especially generational curses) are released upon a person or family, it goes from the head down. Generational curses are passed down from generation to generation to generation. Jesus wore the crown of thorns upon His head so that you can declare that, *"The Curse Stops Here."* The *"HERE"* I am referring to is Jesus Christ. He is the ***"HEAD"*** *of the church* (1 Cor 11:3). When He wore the crown of thorns upon His head He was declaring that the curse stops with Him—the head. If you are born-again and covered by the blood of Jesus Christ, you can boldly declare, "The Curse Stops "**HERE, with the blood of Jesus Christ.**"

So again, Jesus wore the crown of thorns upon His head to dramatically show that He had put an end to the curse of the thorns and thistles from the head down. And, since we are in Christ, the curse stops at the head (Jesus

Christ and the cross) and therefore cannot touch our lives.

The Purpose for the Cross

As you have learned thus far, Jesus paid a high price in order to redeem us and set us free from the curse. But even before Jesus went to the cross, He had already suffered severely and tremendously. He had already been beaten, spat upon, punched, had His beard pulled out, and abused by the Jews the night He was arrested. He endured the tortuous flogging of the Romans while tied to a whipping post. In this torture, His body was beaten and mutilated beyond recognition (Isaiah 52:14).

We saw in the previous topic that after the flogging, the Romans also took a crown of thorns and mashed them into His scalp, causing His blood to be further shed and stream down his face. To this point, Jesus had already done everything necessary according to the law regarding the Sacrificial Lamb in order to redeem us.

He was the perfect Lamb because He had lived a perfect life without sin. He paid the price for our sins with His sufferings. And, He had shed His blood to blot out our sins and transgressions. At this point, His blood could have been taken and placed on heaven's Mercy Seat, thereby erasing our sins forever. Since everything had been done, why was it still necessary for Jesus to go to the cross and continue to suffer further? The answer is found in the following passage:

> *Christ hath redeemed us from the curse of the law, being made a curse for us: for it is written,* **_Cursed is every one that hangeth on a tree._** *(Gal 3:13)*

37

Throughout the New Testament, the Bible inter-changes the cross with a tree many times. This interchange of these two terms is not to simply refer to them both as being made of wood; it uses them to refer to the Biblical representation of hanging on a tree being a curse.

*...if a man has committed a crime punishable by death and he is put to death, and you hang him on a tree, his body shall not remain all night on the tree, but you shall bury him the same day, **for a hanged man is cursed by God**... Deut. 21:22-23 (ESV)*

The reason why hanging from a tree was considered a curse is because of the violation of Adam with the tree in the Garden of Eden. In the Garden of Eden, the Tree of Life represented the Spirit. But the Tree of Knowledge of Good and Evil represented the law, and man's choice of disobedience and rebellion to God's Word.

When Adam chose to eat from the tree of knowledge of good and evil, he was choosing to disobey and rebel against God. God had spoken and told them that *the day in which you eat from the tree (of knowledge of good and evil), you shall surely die.* Adam died in two ways. First, from that moment on, Adam's body began dying. Even though Adam did not physically die until well over 900 years later, his body began decaying and dying the moment he disobeyed God and ate from the tree. Secondly, Adam died instantly in the spirit. So, from that point on, anyone who was hung on a tree for crimes of disobeying the law was considered cursed.

In the Jewish culture and under Jewish law, the punishment for most capital offenses was stoning to death.

Some cases that involved blatant witchcraft could cause someone to be burned to death. But the usual form of capital punishment would be stoning. If a person committed an extremely vile and atrocious crime, the Sanhedrin could order their execution and hanging. The dead body would be hung in public as a deterrent to others for further crime. The hanging of the criminal's body signified more than just a deterrent to crime. It also signified that the person was cursed. It represented a curse that was judged by the law, and it therefore, represented a curse by God—the lawgiver. Again, the reason why hanging someone from a tree represented a curse was because of Adam's defiance to God's Word to disobey and disregard His Word and choose the wrong tree. So if someone was hung on a tree for a crime, the hanging served as a notice to everyone that this person was cursed in the same way that Adam was cursed by choosing the wrong tree and disobeying God.

For he hath made him to be sin for us, who knew no sin; that we might be made the righteousness of God in him. (2 Co 5:21)

By Jesus hanging on the tree (the cross), He became sin for us. God supernaturally transferred the sins of all of mankind onto the body of Jesus Christ. But that's not all of it. God also took the curses that were pronounced upon Adam and mankind in the book of Genesis and placed them upon Jesus while He was on the cross. So, not only did He take our place as sinners, He also took our curses upon His body as well. He became sin and cursed for us at the same time.

After Jesus bore our sins and curses, it became as if Adam and mankind had never sinned. And, the curse that came upon Adam and mankind for choosing the tree of disobedience was removed and placed upon Jesus upon the cross. Again, this is why the New Testament interchanges the cross as the tree. It's because the cross became the cursed tree that Jesus hung on to take our curses that were placed upon us for choosing the cursed tree (of rebellion and disobedience) in the Garden of Eden.

So if Jesus had not gone to the cross, He could have still suffered and paid the price for us our sins, transgressions, and iniquities with his blood, but we still would have been open and susceptible to curses upon our lives. But thanks be to the Lord Jesus Christ that He took our sins and our curses. Therefore, if you are a born-again child of God, then it is unlawful for curses of any kind to be put upon your life or your family lives because the curses were all placed on Jesus.

Double Jeopardy

For God to allow a curse or generational curse upon the life of a born-again Christian would be double jeopardy. In law, double jeopardy is to try a person twice for the same crime. Since Jesus took both the penalty and the curses for us in the court of heavenly judicial righteousness, it would then be unrighteous to allow a curse upon our lives for the same sins and rebelliousness to God's Word that Jesus has already taken and paid for with His own body.

God's Rejection – Our Acceptance

And about the ninth hour Jesus cried with a loud voice, saying, Eli, Eli, lama sabachthani? That is to say, My God, my God, why hast thou forsaken me? (Mat 27:46)

While Jesus hung on the cross, He cried out to God, *"My God, my God, why have You forsaken me?"* He cried this out because for the first time in His existence there was a separation between God the Father and God the Son in the Spirit. God had to separate Himself from Jesus for that moment in time because at that moment Jesus carried all of the sins and all curses of all of mankind.

Since God is Holy, sanctified, and righteous, He cannot be connected to or even in the presence of sin. And, because Jesus became sin and cursed for us, God had to reject Jesus and disconnect His Spirit from His only begotten Son. Because God is all blessings and goodness, He cannot be connected with anyone or anything cursed. So while Jesus carried all of our sins and curses upon His body, God had to reject and forsake Him. There is however a blessing for us through the rejection and forsaking of Jesus by the Father. The blessing is that God forsook and rejected Jesus for a moment so that He would be able to accept and receive us and never forsake us throughout all eternity.

> *To the praise of the glory of his grace, wherein **he hath made us accepted in the beloved**. In whom we have redemption through his blood, the forgiveness of sins, according to the riches of his grace. (Eph 1:6-7)*

Because of the curse, Adam was rejected by God and cast out of the Garden of Eden. Part of the curse was a separation from the Spirit and presence of God. But because Christ took upon His own body our sins and our curses, we are now welcomed and accepted by God. God rejected Jesus for a moment, in order that He may never have to reject us, but rather, openly accept us (through the blood of Jesus Christ). We are now and forever all accepted in the beloved (the presence of God).

Chapter 5

Preparation for the Release

In 2 Samuel Chapter 21,we saw how David and the Israelites experienced a generational curse. We also learned about the role of the Gibeonites and what they represent spiritually. In chapter three, we saw how generational curses were brought upon mankind through Adam's sinful rebellion of God's Word. We also saw many different ways in which Christ has redeemed us from the curse of the law, as well as all curses and generational curses. In this chapter we want to go back and revisit the part of the story that deals with the seven sons of Saul and what they represent, and show how they still pertain to us.

In this story, the seven sons of Saul were a vital part of David and the Israelites receiving their deliverance. If we look closely at how the seven sons of Saul were vital in aiding the deliverance of David and the Israelites, we can take note and use the seven sons of Saul spiritually to aid and assist us in our deliverance from any curse or generational curse.

What Do the Seven Sons of Saul Represent?

Wherefore David said unto the Gibeonites, What shall I do for you? And wherewith shall I make the atonement, that ye may bless the inheritance of the LORD? ***And the Gibeonites said unto him… let seven men of his sons be delivered unto us, and we will hang them*** *up unto the LORD in Gibeah of Saul, whom the LORD did choose. And the king said, I will give them. (2 Samuel 21:3-4)*

In chapter two we said that the Gibeonites represent the spirit of injustice that rises up and cries out to God for retribution when a gross crime has been committed and gone unpaid or unpunished. Since it is usually a great offense that causes someone to desire, ask for, or seek revenge and vengeance, we can then conclude that the spirit of the Gibeonites also represents a great offense against a person or a group of people.

In the above passage, the seven sons of Saul were sacrificed in order to appease the Gibeonites so that they would release the offense from the Israelites. Understanding this, we can then also conclude that the seven sons of Saul represent seven sacrifices that must be made whenever there is a great offense in order for us to get a release.

From chapter three and four, we know now that the blood of Jesus Christ is the ultimate and final sacrifice that is needed to atone for any sin, transgression, or trespass. However, there are some things that God requires us to do in order to obtain His blessings and covering when there is an offense made. The seven sons of Saul represent seven principles of forgiveness and release which must be sacrificed when there is a great offense. I used the word *"sacrificed"* for two reasons: First, because in the story, they were sacrificed (hung) to avenge the offense of Saul. Secondly, I used the word *"sacrifice"* because it is always a sacrifice of the soul to obey God and resist the warring and pride of the flesh. And, just as David and the Israelites received the healing of their land once the sacrifice was completed, you will also receive healing in your life, family, or generation once they have been sacrificed.

The Seven Sons of Saul
—the Seven Principles of Release

1. Repent, and ask God to forgive you for your sins
2. Repent of the sins of your ancestors
3. Forgive others of their offenses against you
4. Release others of their offenses against you
5. Apologize to the person whom you have offended
6. Cut off and repent of sins that opens doors to Satan
7. Appropriate the blood of Jesus Christ to your life and family

Do I Have to Sacrifice All Seven Sons?

The above seven things represent seven things that must be done in order to get a spiritual and physical release in the case of an egregious offense. These are not outdated Old Testament laws which are no longer observed. They are principles of offense, release, and forgiveness that are even taught in the New Testament by our Lord, Jesus Christ, Himself. Only one of them is an Old Testament principle.

The remaining six are thoroughly taught throughout the New Testament. If you suspect that either you or a family member could be in some type of reoccurring curse, generational curse, or stronghold over your life, I strongly suggest that you do what David did.

First, diligently seek the Lord for an answer and the directions that He would have you to take. If you do not get a clear clarion answer from the Lord as to the source of the problem, I strongly encourage you to do what David and the Israelites did and sacrifice all the seven sons of Saul.

The Mechanic

At this point, I know that many of you may be saying this: After seeing these seven principles of offense, you can see how several of them may be applicable to help give you a release and set you free when there is a great offense. But some may refuse to acknowledge the need to use or sacrifice all seven of them. To that point, I have this story:

One day, my car began to run hot. After consulting with a mechanic, I was told that it was one of several things: the radiator cap, water pump, the thermostat, or antifreeze. After several tests, we narrowed it down to the water pump as the more likely culprit of the problem. I was also told by the mechanic that I should replace all of them since the other items were very easy and inexpensive to replace. In my haste to get back on the road, I replaced the water pump but put off the other three things, planning to do them at a later time, but never did. Sometime later, I ended up having another leak—this time it was the thermostat. By this time it (a ten dollar thermostat) had caused a much more serious problem that ended up costing me fifteen hundred dollars in repairs.

I said all that to say that the seven sons of Saul are very easy things to do. Most people would be willing to replace the water pump—which may represent the more obvious spiritual things to do such as pleading the blood of Jesus Christ and binding and losing the devil. But if God has given us these principles of release from an offense, why not just do what our heavenly mechanic has instructed us to do, and replace all the items (sacrifice all seven sons of Saul). My failure to listen to the mechanic ended up costing me fifteen hundred dollars. Your failure to listen to the instructions of our (heavenly) mechanic may cost you years of unnecessary difficulties and struggles in your life, family, or generation.

When these seven things are done and maintained in your life, they will clear the atmosphere, clear your heart, mind, and spirit, and prepare you to receive the blessings of God and the covering of the Lord after there has been a great offense.

As you do these seven things and carry each of them out, you will be able to see and sense the release and freedom in the spirit, a reconnection with the Spirit of God, and a removal of hindrances and strongholds that has bound and held you back as a result of the offense.

Chapter 6

The Seven Sons of Saul

1. Repent of Your Sins

If they shall confess their iniquity... which they trespassed against me, and that also they have walked contrary unto me... Then will I remember my covenant with Jacob, and also my covenant with Isaac, and also my covenant with Abraham will I remember; and I will remember the land. (Leviticus 26:40-42)

The first principal of release of the seven sons of Saul is that we confess our sins and iniquities unto God. Again, this is not solely an Old Testament commandment. It is a New Testament requirement as well. In this passage, God says that if we would confess our sins unto Him, that He would remember His covenant with Abraham concerning us.

When a person becomes born-again, through Christ, they become the spiritual seed of Abraham. It was through

Abraham that God chose to establish His covenant. In a sense, when we become born-again, we become spiritual Jews. So when God says He will remember the covenant He made with Abraham, Isaac, and Jacob, He is also referring to the covenant He made with us (the spiritual seed of Abraham). This covenant includes God's promise to bless us, protect us, have mercy upon us, and forgive us. But all this is contingent upon the first part, which is to confess our sins.

Yes—our sins are covered by the blood of Jesus Christ. But the covering of the blood of Jesus is contingent upon our truthful and heartfelt confession to God of our sins.

For the word of God is quick, and powerful, and sharper than any two-edged sword, piercing even to the dividing asunder of soul and spirit, and of the joints and marrow, and is a discerner of the thoughts and intents of the heart. (Heb 4:12)

If the Holy Spirit brings a sin up to your spirit that you have committed, repent of it and ask God to cover it with the Blood. It may be something that happened during the past hour, day, week or month. It may even be something that happened years ago. If it is something that keeps bothering you over and over again, it is possibly something that has not been completely and adequately repented of and dealt with from the heart. Sometimes, we can say things from head knowledge of what we should do without truly dealing with the heart.

The Holy Spirit is the only true discerner of the thoughts, intents, and meditations of the heart. The more we read the Word of God and yield to the Holy Spirit, the more God will reveal the truth to us about our actions, words, and deeds. And, the more He will deal with us concerning our sins until we repent of them.

Whosoever is born of God doth not commit sin; for his seed remaineth in him: and he cannot sin, because he is born of God. (1 John 3:9)

For many years I had a hard time understanding this passage. I knew I had been born-again, but I also knew that there had been times in my Christian life where I had sinned. This passage made it sound as if anyone who committed sin was not truly born-again. It caused me to question the confidence of my salvation for many years until God gave me the revelation of this passage.

What this passage is actually saying is that a person who is born-again cannot continually commit sin and live with sin in their heart without the conviction of the Holy Spirit. Because the Spirit of truth abides within us, the spirit of sin and iniquity cannot comfortably abide in us. Sin and iniquity will continue to convict and bother a true child of God until they confess and repent of it to God.

As a true child of God, you cannot grossly, consciously, and knowingly offend or hurt people without it bothering you and convicting your heart. If you can offend people, hurt them, or do them wrong and it does not bother your conscious, something is wrong somewhere. In Hebrews 12:6-7 the Bible says that God brings conviction on those whom He loves. This is why God will not leave us alone with sin—because He loves us. But when you bring it to the surface and confess and repent of it, your conscious becomes clear and the Holy Spirit brings peace to your heart.

Conviction vs. Condemnation

There are times when we have truly confessed our sins from our heart and our conscious continues to bring it back up to us over and over again. This may be a case where the devil is using the spirit of condemnation in your life.

The spirit of condemnation is a spirit from Satan that attempts to keep you in the bondage and stronghold of guilt and shame. Conviction makes us feel condemned, but it brings us to a place of true repentance. Once you sincerely and genuinely repent from your heart to God, He no longer holds you in the spirit of condemnation. It is the devil that does that. If the devil is attempting to hold you as a prisoner of condemnation long after you have repented, you need to renew your mind in the faith of God's mercy and forgiveness. Begin reading and confessing scriptures that deal with Christ redeeming us and shedding His blood for us on the cross. As you continue doing this, you will eventually get a release, and you will begin to know in your heart that you have been forgiven, cleansed, and totally delivered by God from that offense.

2. Repent of the Sins of your Ancestors

*If they shall confess their iniquity, **and the iniquity of their fathers, with their trespass which they trespassed against me**, and that also they have walked contrary unto me...* (Leviticus 26:40-42)

There are some who say that because we are in Christ, the sins of the fathers have no effect on the children. There are others who say that the sins of the fathers do affect the children and that we need to heed to them, be aware of them accordingly, and repent of them. There are scriptures on both sides that either endorse or disavow each view.

Scriptures such as Deut. 24:16, Jeremiah 31:29-30, Ezekiel 18:1-4 seem to endorse the first, and scriptures like Exodus 20:5-6, Jeremiah 32:18, Nehemiah 9:2, Leviticus 26:40 seem to endorse the latter. Well, if the Bible does not contradict itself, then what does that mean? I believe that it means both. I believe that our nation, generation, family's lives and our lives are in some way affected by the sins of our fathers. But I also believe that if we are born-again and properly covered by the blood of Jesus Christ, and we properly repent of our sins, and the sins of the fathers, that God will exempt us from the effects of the sins of the fathers.

It's like being a Christian citizen of the United States. Individually, we may not be personally responsible for the moral decay and degradation of our nation. When we stand before God, He will not judge us personally for how we have fallen away from God as a nation. However, the actions of our parents, ancestors, and forefathers who have allowed and even endorsed the sins and abominations of our nation to bring it to the debase state we are now in can have an effect upon and influence our present lives. Again, God does not hold us personally responsible for their sins, and we will not be judged by them. However, the influence of their sins now affects the grace, protection, blessings, and prosperity of God concerning our present nation, which in return affects the circumstances and condition of each of our lives personally.

It's the same with curses and generational curses. We may not be responsible for the sins and spiritual rebellion of our parents and ancestors against God, and God will not hold us accountable for them and neither will we be judged for them. However, their spirit of sin and rebellion can have an effect upon the lifestyle, situations and circumstances of our lives and family as a whole, which includes us, and our present families and how we live and what we go through.

Repenting as an Intercessor

When you repent on behalf of your nation, city, family, community, race, and so on, you are interceding on behalf of that group of people unto God. In Ezekiel 22:30, God said that He was looking for a man or woman that would *"make up the hedge and stand in the gap."* To stand in the gap is to serve as a go between. To do this, you must in some way identify with the people for which you are standing in the gap.

In Deut 9:13-14 God became angry with the Israelites because of their rebellion, and told Moses that He was going to destroy them and begin a great nation again with Moses. Moses put himself in harm's way (by standing in the way when God was angry) and interceded on behalf of the Israelites, and God spared them because of Moses' intercession.

Moses interceded before God on behalf of the sins of the people, but yet he included himself among them. He was willing to suffer with them because of their sins, rather than be excluded from them. When you repent as an intercessor you are doing the exact same thing Moses did. This is what you are doing when you repent as an intercessor. You include yourself among those whom you are praying and interceding for as one with them—while repenting and asking for God's mercy and forgiveness.

Through the cross, Jesus became sin for us—thereby identifying with us. When you identify with them, through your prayers, intercession, and repentance, you are standing in the gap on their behalf.

When you intercede for the sins and iniquities of a group of people that you are connected to, you don't exclude yourself from them, you include yourself with them. You don't include yourself with them with sin, but rather, as an intercessor. It's like you are including yourself in the group and saying to God that all of us have sinned, and we are all asking You to have mercy on all of us and forgive and cleanse us all.

The following are men of God who stood in the gap and interceded in the Bible. They all interceded on behalf of the sins of Israel. These were all righteous men who had not done the type of sins for which they were interceding. But in order to stand in the gap between them and God, they identified themselves with an ungodly people.

- Isaiah expressed his heartfelt repentance on behalf of his nation of Israel (Is 6:5).

- Jeremiah acknowledges the wickedness of his generation and ancestors (Jer 14:20).

- Daniel repented of the sins of his nation when he heard of the devastation of Jerusalem (Daniel 9:20).

- Nehemiah repented on behalf of the sins of his nation (Neh 1:6).

Again, all of these were righteous men. But when they repented to God, they didn't ask God to forgive *"them"* for *their* sins, they asked God to forgive *"us"* for *"our"* sins. Another reason why it is necessary to identify with the sins of the fathers when you are asking God to forgive them is that you are not perfect. Your sins may not be as numerous or spiritually dreadful as the sins of others, but they are still nonetheless sins. Jesus said that we cannot look at the mote in our brother's eye when there is something in our own eye. When you look down on the sins of others in judgment, the sin of pride is not that far away.

It's hard to ask God to forgive us for the sins of our nation and the sins of our ancestors when we ourselves have had sin and transgressions in our lives. So when you are repenting for the sins of your ancestors and family line, include yourself. Do as the patriarchs above did. Include yourself among them in your repentance. When you pray this way, you are eliminating the spirit of pride in your own heart and life, and you are covering the entire family line.

Just in Case

Another reason why you would stand in the gap and intercede for the sins of a group of people is this: Although you might be able to claim that individually you are born-again, covered by the blood of Jesus Christ, and have not sinned, everyone in your family or group may not be as right with God as you are. What about the other members of your family and even your children or grandchildren who may not be born-again, walking in obedience and integrity with God, or properly walking under the canopy of God's protection. If they are not, then they are still liable to these curses and generational curses.

There are times when it becomes necessary to repent for your entire family on behalf of your ancestors just in case one or some of them is not in the place with God that they should be.

And it was so, when the days of their feasting were gone about, that Job sent and sanctified them, and rose up early in the morning, and offered burnt offerings according to the number of them all: for Job said, It may be that my sons have sinned, and cursed God in their hearts. Thus did Job continually. (Job 1:5)

In this passage Job made sacrifices continually on behalf of his children, *"just in case."* The Bible says that Job did this continually, *"just in case"* they had sinned or cursed God in their heart.

You may be able to account for your life and actions, but you cannot actually account for people whom you are unaware of their daily and hourly actions. So there is nothing wrong with asking God to have mercy upon your children and family and forgive them of their sins, and to also repent of the sins of your ancestors and declare that their sins shall not touch your family members and children. When you repent on behalf of your ancestors, you are covering your entire family just in case they are not right with God or they are not properly covered by the blood of Jesus Christ.

It's like you are carrying an extra insurance policy upon them so that they will have extra insurance coverage and avert any kind of curse that could be coming down the bloodline on behalf of your ancestors.

Remember, curses and generational curses are real and can come upon members of your family who are unaware of the truth of the Gospel of Jesus Christ. Let's do like Job and cover our families and repent of our sins, our family's sins, and the sins of our ancestors, ***"Just in Case."***

3. Forgive Others for their Offenses Against You

We have shown through Leviticus 26:40-42 that in order to get released from generational curses, you must first confess your sins, and then confess the sins of your ancestors. The next step is to release forgiveness.

Matthew 18:23-27

The above scripture reference is a parable of a king who called his servants to accountability. Upon doing so, he discovered that one of his stewards had been cheating him and stealing his money. The king then ordered this man, along with his entire family to be put in prison. The man then begged the king's forgiveness and pleaded with him to have mercy. The king was so touched with the man humbling himself and apologizing for his wrong that he forgave the man and gave him another chance. On top of that, the king even cleared the man's debts, leaving him now owing nothing.

Matthew 18:28-34

The above scripture reference is the remainder of the parable. Shortly after the king forgave his steward of the debt owed him, this same steward found another man who also owed him money. The steward treated the man harshly, grabbing him by the throat and threatened to put him in jail if he didn't pay the money owed to him. The man then began to plea for mercy to the steward the same way the steward had done to the king. But instead of him showing the man the same mercy and forgiveness that the king had shown him, he put the man in prison to pay the debt.

The king soon heard of this incident and became enraged. He was enraged because he had forgiven the steward of his debt and spared him and his family from going to prison, but yet this same steward had not shown any mercy to someone else who likewise owed him money. The king then withdrew the pardon he had given the steward and had him put in prison.

The first point that I want to bring out about this passage is that not only was the steward in danger of going to jail because of the debt he owed the king, but his entire family was also in danger of being imprisoned. The steward's spouse and children did not personally steal the king's money, but because of their relation to this steward, they were tied to him, and were therefore made responsible for suffering the punishment along with the steward. In the same manner, a generational curse can be executed against someone who did not actually commit a particular sin, but simply because of their family or generational relationship to the person. Again, this only applies to people who are not born-again and properly covered by the blood of Jesus Christ. When we fail to forgive others of their offenses and trespasses against us, we risk the same as the steward did. We risk the anger of "The King,"

...As We Forgive Our Debtors

The second point I want to bring out is this: When someone sins or transgress against you (according to the Spirit and Word of God), they become indebted to you. This is why in the Lord's prayer, God instructs us to ask for forgiveness for our sins (debts), as we forgive our debtors (those who have sinned against or offended us).

You, therefore, become responsible for either releasing the debt (forgiving them) or holding them responsible to pay the penalty for the debt or transgression. As long as you refuse to forgive them, they are held in a type of spiritual debt to you. This spiritual debt is a type of spiritual prison. As long as they are in this spiritual prison, it gives the spiritual Gibeonites the right to judge them.

In the story with David, the Gibeonites refused to release and forgive the Israelites until the offense had been judged. In the same manner, when a person refuses to forgive someone of a transgression or offense against them, it can possibly hold them in a type of spiritual prison that allows the judgment of the Gibeonites to be executed upon their life, family, or generation. I believe that this is the reason why some sins and transgressions are judged (in this life) and why some are not judged.

If the offended person dies without ever forgiving and releasing the person, the spirit of the Gibeonites continues to rise up before God crying for judgment even long after their death.

Many generational curses have been executed because an offense was made against an individual or family, and the offended person refused to forgive and release them. The longer the person is held in unforgiveness, the longer this spirit cries out to God for vengeance and judgment until they are finally judged.

This does not mean that every offense that is unforgiven will be judged. God declares in Romans 12:19 that vengeance belongs to Him. God is the one who decides if He will listen to the cry of the spiritual Gibeonites or not. However, there are some that God will hear and allow. The greater the sin or offense, the louder they cry. Also, the greater the sin or offense, the longer they cry—meaning, from generation to generation. This is the reason why certain sins and transgressions such as murder, rape, sexual perversions, abominations, and abuse (physical, emotional or sexual), are often judged in one form or another, in one generation or another.

What Comes Around Goes Around

"What comes around goes around" is a street adage that carries the same meaning as the biblical account of ***"you will reap what you sow."*** In the previous topic we discovered that when someone offends or trespasses against you, you have the right to hold them in unforgiveness. And, as long as they are held in unforgiveness (a type of spiritual prison), the spirit of the Gibeonites can begin to rise up and ask God for vengeance. And, the more severe the crime, sin or offense, the longer and louder they will cry for vengeance.

This type of spiritual prison, however, works both ways. When you refuse to forgive someone for an offense, not only does it allow the spirit of the Gibeonites to rise up and ask for vengeance upon them and their descendants' lives, it also opens the door for them to begin to rise up and ask for vengeance and justice upon your life and descendants as well. As long as you hold someone in the spiritual prison of unforgiveness, the spirit of the Gibeonites can also judge you for offenses you have made against others. But that's not all. It allows the spirit of the Gibeonites to also execute judgment against you for offenses that were made by your ancestors. This is why Jesus taught on forgiveness so much. It wasn't just because it's the right Christian thing to do; it's also because of what unforgiveness does to you.

Some people become so angered and enraged over an offense against them that they feel that they can never release forgiveness. But you have got to let it go—not just for the person's sake, but for your own sake and the sake of your family and descendants.

Allowing the Sun to Set

Be ye angry, and sin not: let not the sun go down upon your wrath: Neither give place to the devil. (Eph 4:26-27)

The above passage is referencing the point that we should not give any place to the devil in our lives. This passage says that we give place to the devil when we allow the sun to go down upon our wrath (anger). It's not saying that you sin by simply getting angry. There is no one who has ever lived who didn't get angry at something. But it's what happens after you get angry that determines whether or not you sin and give place to Satan in your life. The sin comes in when you let the sun go down on your wrath. Letting the sun go down upon your wrath is to hold on to the anger day after day, week after week, and even year after year, never choosing to forgive and let it go.

I once heard of two sisters who were very close until (while teenagers) one of them slept with the other's boyfriend. This ignited a feud between them that lasted for fifty years. It actually lasted until they finally died. They died, never reconciling with each other, allowing this offense to destroy what should have been 50 years of sisterly love.

The Poison

When you allow the anger of an offense to enter into your heart, and you sleep on it night after night, day after day, week after week, and so on, it begins to cause your heart to become infected. It's like a wound that is not properly cleaned that begins to develop infection and fester pus.

At this point, the person's mind, heart, and soul become open to hear the voice and suggestions of Satan. He begins speaking to their heart, reminding them of the offense over and over again. The more they think about it, the more angered and enraged they become, and the more infected their heart also becomes.

The next stage is that this infection of their heart now enters their spirit, and their spirit becomes poisoned. Once a person's spirit becomes poisoned, it changes their character, countenance, and disposition. Unfortunately, there are many people who go to church every Sunday who have poisoned spirits. When you meet them at first, they may seem loving and pleasant; but after a while, the poison in their spirit begins to ooze out and becomes noticeable to many people.

Once a person's spirit becomes poisoned, it begins affecting other areas of their lives as well. It affects their lives spiritually, socially, emotionally, and even physically. It affects them spiritually because they can never really get into the holy presence of God with a poisoned spirit. They can come to church, sing hymns, and go through all types of religious motions, but they can never have true worship, fellowship, or intimacy with God. It affects them socially because they have trouble establishing and maintaining relationships and friendships both romantically and socially. It affects them emotionally because it hides and buries their true, inner emotions—allowing only a false shell of who they really are to be seen. It affects them physically because once this poison gets down inside their spirit, because the spirit and body are so closely connected, it begins to corrode the body in the form of sickness and disease.

Trace It, Face It, and Erase It

At this point the person needs either a psychiatrist or a pastor who understands curses, generational curses, and poisoned spirits. A psychiatrist gets paid a lot of money to go into your past, find the poison, and help root it out. In order to dig this kind of poison out, you have to do three things: ***trace it, face it, and erase it.***

The psychiatrist or minister has to go back into your past to find the root. Many times they have to go all the way back to your childhood. They will get the person to talk about their parents, other relatives, friends, and relationships.

They will go from your childhood, to high school, and on to adulthood. Somewhere hidden in their life is a root of offense that has never been properly dealt with and has festered and poisoned their spirit. This is the "trace it" part—locating the offense. When they locate it, there is a trigger that goes off in the person. The person's whole facial expression, countenance, attitude, and sometimes even their voice level and modulation changes. Some psychiatrist will even put a type of lie detector apparatus on the patient that measures their pulse during this time. When the psychiatrist hits the root, the person's pulse will even rise. This lets them know they have hit the root.

The next step is to face it. They get the person to face

the fact that this person or situation has injured them. This is sometimes difficult because there are times that the offense has been there so long and hidden so deep that the person does not even realize that it bothers them deep down on the inside as much as it does.

Finally, the last step is to erase it. To erase it just simply means to forgive the person for the offense. Sometimes it is hard for the offended person to release forgiveness. But the psychiatrist lets them know that continuing to hold on to this offense will only continue harm, hinder, and hurt them in life. They also remind them that it is much better for them to forgive the person for their own sake. After it has been forgiven (erased), the next step is to release it.

4. Release Others of Their Offenses Against You

Many people do not understand the difference between forgiveness and release. Many think that when you forgive someone, that you are also automatically releasing them. Although they are very similar and close, there is a difference. Forgiveness is a choice of your will. Releasing someone is an action and condition of the heart. When I say that forgiveness is a choice of your will, it's something that you choose to do out of your conscious will. You can choose to forgive someone because you know the spiritual harm it will do to you if you hold on to unforgiveness. But releasing them from your heart takes more than mere words.

There are times that an offense is relatively mild, and the choice you make to forgive them can also produce a release in your heart for them. But there are also other offenses that are so severe, and the scars and wounds from the offense are so deep, that even though you choose to forgive them, it may take time and effort to fully release them from your heart. The offended person may want to release them, but the severity of the pain from the offense causes them to indirectly hold on to the offense long after words of forgiveness may have been uttered.

The Total Release

In our previous topic, we discovered that if we fail to both forgive and release someone, it holds them in spiritual prison and causes them to become vulnerable to the judgment of the spiritual Gibeonites. We also discovered that it not only holds them in spiritual prison, it also holds us in spiritual prison as well. And, while we are in spiritual prison, we also become vulnerable to the judgment of the spiritual Gibeonites, not only for our sins, but also for our ancestors' sins. This is why it is so important for you to learn not only to forgive people who have offended you, but also to seek the Lord until you get a total release. The release is not only for them, it's just as much for you.

If you think you may have been under a curse or generational curse, you must ask the Holy Spirit to help you to search your heart to see if there is anyone in your life who has wounded you with a severe offense that you have not been able to totally release. You may have said you forgave them, or may have even told the person you forgave them, but yet in your heart you have not truly released them yet.

In the cases where the wounds and scars of the offense are deep and debilitating, the person needs the supernatural help of the Holy Spirit to help them to actually release the person. When someone has deeply wounded us, we often cover the offense by attempting to forget it as quickly as we can. Time can help us to cover the offense where the sting and pain no longer bother us as bad, but underneath the cover, the offense is still as strong. All it takes is a moderate reminder of the incident, and the emotional pain and agony of the offense resurface. Although you may want to release them, the severity of the wound causes your heart to continue to hold on to the offense. Without the supernatural intervention and help of the Holy Spirit, you may hold on to this offense for the rest of your life, even though you may have said you forgave the person.

One of the ways you can tell whether or not you have truly released a person from a major offense is if it terribly bothers or grieves you to be around the offender, think about them, or even hear their name mentioned. If their name or presence still bothers or grieves you, you may have only covered up the offense and may need to get a release.

Another way you can tell if you are still suffering from the wounds of an offense is if you have a deep desire for them to get rewarded for what they did to you. I often hear people say, *"they did me wrong, but they are going to get theirs."* They say this in regard to an offender, hoping that God will reward them evil (pay them back) for the wrong or transgression done to them. If you have thought, said, or even hoped this for someone who has offended you, then you have not truly released them.

> *And they stoned Stephen, calling upon God, and saying, Lord Jesus, receive my spirit. And he kneeled down, and cried with a loud voice, Lord, <u>lay not this sin to their charge</u>. And when he had said this, he fell asleep [died]. (Acts 7:59-60)*

In this passage they stoned Stephen for preaching the Gospel of Jesus Christ. While dying, he asked the Lord not to lay this sin to their charge. He was in essence asking God to not only forgive and release them from this sin, but to also not even cause anything to happen to them as payback for their transgression against him.

Again, when you speak, desire, or hope someone gets paid back for an offense against you, you have not truly released them. You may be speaking forgiveness out of your mouth, but from your heart you are seeking revenge.

Father, Forgive them...

When Jesus was on the cross, He asked God to forgive those who had made Him to suffer and those who had crucified Him. He did this for two reasons. First, He knew that they did not believe or realize they had actually brutally tortured and murdered the Son of the Living God. He knew that the payment for this sin would have severely cursed their descendants for centuries to come. Now even though they still had to pay the eternal penalty for their sins, Christ's forgiveness released and spared them and their descendants from some devastating curses.

The second reason He did it was because He could not go to the grave in the spirit of offense. In our previous topic, we quoted Ephesians 4:26-27 that tells us *not to give place to the devil by allowing the sun to go down upon our wrath*. People who die holding on to offenses by intentionally refusing to both forgive and release others, place themselves in a very dangerous position when they stand before God. It's dangerous because of this: God forgives and covers our sins based upon us forgiving and releasing the sins of others.

When we realize that our sins are connected with the forgiveness and release of the sins and offense of others

against us, it makes it altogether easier to forgive and release them. But in spite of knowing this, there are people
who still choose to go to the grave intentionally refusing to
forgive and release others. Those who do so risk standing
before God and having to stand accountable to God for
their sins, and thereby risk their eternal salvation.

Prayer—the Key to the Release

In 1979 one of my brothers was brutally shot and murdered by someone. Although the person was guilty beyond
a shadow of doubt, they only did a couple of years in
prison. After I became born-again, I learned that I must
forgive everyone, so I forgave them. But even though I said
that I forgave this person, I didn't discover until years later
that I still held on to the offense of them killing my brother.
I didn't realize this until I came in contact with that person
again after many years. Even though I wanted to release
them, it was very difficult to do so.

I later began seeking the Lord as to how I could totally
release them. It was then that God gave me the well-known
passage in Matthew 5:44 which tells us to "***pray for them
which despitefully use us and persecute us.***" At that
time this was something that I definitely did not feel like
doing. But I did not do it because I wanted to; I did it because I knew I needed to.

Prayer produces intimacy. When you pray, you become
intimate with the One you are praying to (God), the one
you are praying with, and the one you are praying for.
When you spend time praying for someone, the intimacy of
your prayers begins to pull down the walls of offense. The
more you pray for them, the more the spirit of God begins
to mend your heart and help you to totally and fully release

them.

After the Lord showed me this, I began praying for them on a routine basis. I will not lie; it took some time. But as I continued to pray for them, eventually, the grievous walls of offense came down, and I was able to truly release them from the offense from my heart. In fact, I was later able to talk with them on several occasions and not feel any anger, resentment or ill-will in my heart towards them. This was done through the power of prayer and the Word of God. The Word of God transforms both our heart and our minds.

Again, prayer is the key to getting a total release from the spirit of offense. If the Holy Spirit reveals someone in your past to you that you have not both forgiven and released, begin praying for them until you get a total release. Pray for their salvation. Pray for God's blessings upon their life. And, pray for God's mercy and forgiveness. As you continue to pray for them, the walls of offense will become broken down and you will get the total release from your heart and spirit.

The key in this prayer is not so much what you are saying as much as what you are doing. It's the process of you praying for them that generates the spiritual intimacy that causes the release. Put them on your prayer list to pray for them once a week or however often the Lord leads you until you sense the total release.

* Note: God commands us to forgive and release those who have offended us, but He never commanded us to blindly trust or put ourselves in a dangerous or vulnerable position with them again. Use the wisdom of the Spirit of God.

5. Apologize to the Person You Have Offended

Wherefore David said unto the Gibeonites, __What shall I do for you? and wherewith shall I make the atonement__, that ye may bless the inheritance of the LORD? (2 Samuel 21:3)

Humble Yourself and Go to the Source

After David sought the face of the Lord, God gave him the answer of what to do about the famine which had been upon them for three years. In the above passage, you find David going to the Gibeonites and asking them what he could do to make it right with them.

The point I want to bring out in this passage is that although David was the mighty king of Israel, and the Gibeonites were only servants to the Israelites, he had to humble himself and go to the Gibeonites and make it right with them in order to get the curse removed.

David didn't refuse to do it because he was the king. He knew that his position had nothing to do with what he needed to do. He knew that humbling his heart and apologizing to the Gibeonites (even though the Gibeonites were their servants) was the only way to get released from the curse. Just as David didn't let his pride keep him from humbling his heart and making it right, don't let your pride keep you from humbling yourself and making it right with someone whom you may have offended.

If you know of a severe offense that you have committed against someone, or the Holy Spirit reveals to you a severe offense you have committed against someone, you must humble your heart and go to them and apologize and make it right.

That You May Be Healed...

Confess your faults one to another, and pray one for another, <u>that ye may be healed</u>... (James 5:16)

Several church denominations have incorrectly interpreted this passage to mean that when you have sinned, you must go to a pastor or priest to confess your sins to them. But that is not what this passage is referring to. It is referring to the case of someone making a great offense against someone humbling yourself and going to them and confess and apologize to the person you have offended. Now look at the underlined part of this passage where it says, **"*that ye may be healed.*"** When you go to the source (the offended person) and make it right with them, healing takes place. David's land was healed because he went to the source and made it right. Likewise, when you go to the source and make it right with them, you will receive healing in your life, health, family or situation.

There is a saying that says "Confession is good for the soul." There is a lot of truth in that saying. One of the reasons why confessing your faults to someone whom you have offended brings healing is because it releases the soul from spiritual toxicity.

When the spirit of offense takes place, Satan is right there involved in the midst of it. He stirs the actions of one to offend on one side, and then he stirs the heart of offense on the other side. If no one releases the offense, the toxicity of the offense begins to build up in the spiritual realm until it explodes under pressure. When you go to the source and make it right, it's like letting the air out of a pressurized tank thereby relieving the pressure.

Leave thy Gift at the Altar

Therefore if thou bring thy gift to the altar, and there rememberest that thy brother hath ought against thee; <u>leave there thy gift before the altar, and go thy way; first be reconciled to thy brother, and then come and offer thy gift</u>. --Matthew 5:23-24

Holding on to offenses is not only a danger and a hindrance to your well-being and surroundings, it is also a danger to your relationship with God. Jesus was teaching us here that while a person is in the spirit of offense, God does not hear their prayers, receive their worship, or receive their offerings and sacrifices until they go to the person involving the offense and make it right with them.

Notice where it says, *"If thy brother hath an ought against thee..."* With God, it doesn't matter who is at fault. Whether it's your fault or the other person's fault is not as important to God as the spirit involving the offense. It's like when a mother has two children that are fighting and at odds with each other, the mother is more concerned about them coming together in love and unity that she is about who's right and who's wrong. The two siblings may be more concerned about the rights and wrongs of the argument or discord, but the mother is only concerned about ending the fighting and arguing with one another.

It's the same reasoning with the Holy Spirit. When the spirit of discord and offense is upon someone, the Holy Spirit will not rest upon their spirit and flow through them. God is love and peace. And, His Spirit will not rest upon and flow through a vessel when the vessel is filled with strife and discord.

God is not looking for you to take the total blame when there is contention or discord among the brethren, but remember, *"It takes two to tango."* You must be at least willing clear the atmosphere and get your spirit right and at peace. You may need to go and apologize for the part you played and how you handled the contention or discord. This often times leads to both parties coming together and totally apologizing and repenting to one another.

The Right Kind of Apology

If the Holy Spirit deals with your heart about an offense you have made against someone, and you are led to go and make it right, first, be prayerful about it. Ask God to intervene and deal with your heart as well as prepare the heart of the other person before you go to them. Then, if you must make an apology, make sure the apology is sincere, heartfelt, and authentic. If the person does not feel that the apology was authentic, they will either not be willing to amend the situation or will choose to continue to hold on the spirit of offense.

When someone apologizes to another person, most people with any type of adult maturity will forgive them. If the offense was really severe to them, you may have to sit there and listen to them tell you how much it hurt them. If they do this, do not attempt to justify yourself or give reasons for the offense; just continue to be apologetic until you are finished. David didn't make any excuses for the actions of Saul against the Gibeonites, he just accepted the responsibility and did as they requested. You must do the same.

If you are the person whom someone is apologizing to, remember that we have all made mistakes. And, just as they offended or hurt you, that you have offended and hurt others at times in your life. Also remember that our offense against God and His laws and Word far outweigh someone else's offenses against us. And, just as Christ has forgiven us, we must also be willing to forgive others.

What If They Will Not Forgive You?

If it be possible, as much as lieth in you, live peaceably with all men. (Romans 12:18)

Finally, brethren, pray for us... that we may be delivered from <u>unreasonable</u> and wicked men: for all men have not faith. (2 Thessalonians 3:1-2)

There are situations where the offended person may (because of the severity of the offense to them) choose to strongly hold on to the hurt or offense and not want to see the person who offended them, speak to them, or have anything whatsoever to do with them. And, some would rather die and take it to the grave with them than to ever even think about forgiving the person who offended them.

These two passages cover these types of situations. The first passage tells us to do it (go to them) **"*if it is possible.*"** It may not be possible to reconcile in peace with some people because of their intense anger and resentment concerning the offense. The second passage tells us that there will be some people who will be **"*unreasonable.*"** Another way of describing someone who is unreasonable is a person who refuses to reason. These two types of people may not want to accept your apology or attempt to reconcile a peaceful relationship.

Because they refuse to forgive, release, or even come

together does not mean that you are forced to endure their guilt and offense until they choose to do so. Your sincere attempt to go to them to resolve the matter is all that God requires of you.

In Matthew 5:23-24 Jesus did not say that they have to accept your attempt to reconcile with them in peace. If you offended someone, the first step is to go to God and ask for His forgiveness. After that, God instructs us to (humble ourselves) and go to the person and make it right with them. But if they refuse to reconcile with you, or refuse your attempt to apologize to them, then you have done what God commands of you. At that point you are released from God and released from the offense. The only things you have left that you can do at that point is to pray for them that God would someday soften their heart and cause them to be willing to receive forgiveness and release it from their heart.

What If the Person cannot be found or is Deceased?

If you cannot find them or if the person is deceased, then you release the matter totally to God. When you go before God, be sensitive to God's instructions. He may have you to do something specific or even make some type of restitution regarding the offense of the person that is deceased.

In our foundational passage, David went to the Gibeonites' great grandchildren to get a release. This may not work for many. Do not go to children and grandchildren unless the offense is well known throughout the children and grandchildren, and it is a truly egregious offense and you are definitely without a doubt led of the Lord to do so. Most of the time, the children and grandchildren are not even aware of the incident. They, therefore, do not hold the grudge or unforgiveness. If you reveal to them the offense that took place in another generation, it is going to only stir up bitterness, resentment, and strife for you—something they may not have had for you prior to your disclosure. But in David's case, the offense had been passed down to further generations. They were well aware of the offense and held the same bitter anger and hatred towards David and the Israelites for what Saul had done. So in his case, it was necessary to go to the children of the deceased.

Covering a Transgression with Love

Let me give this caution: This point of having to go to the source to make it right has to be done in the wisdom, leading, guidance, and sensitivity of the Holy Spirit.

In order to get their hearts right with God, some people attempt to go back in their lives and confess everything they have done to everyone they have wronged or transgressed. While this is a very noble thing to do, if it is not done by the leading and guidance of the Lord, it can sometimes do more harm than good.

He that covereth a transgression seeketh love; but he that repeateth a matter separateth very friends. (Proverbs 17:9)

There are some things that are better left covered (not revealed or confessed to the person offended or transgressed), rather than to reveal the truth to them. I know this sounds like somewhat of a contradiction to the things we have stated earlier with this point, but it is sometimes necessary.

Let me give you an example of what I am referring to: Let's say that a couple has been married for twenty years. Let's say at this point that they are happy and settled in their marriage and their love for each other. But let's say in year five of their marriage, the man cheated on his wife with another woman. Many would say that this man needs to go to the wife and disclose to her what he did. But that's not always the best thing to do.

He that **covereth a transgression** <u>**seeketh love**</u>*...*

The above passage tells us that sometimes it is necessary to cover a transgression, meaning, keep it covered and not reveal it to them. Now, before you get excited about not having to do this point, you must understand that the motive must be right. The motive of this concealment *"must" be love.* This passage is not for those who simply do not want to be embarrassed, exposed, or humbled; it's for those who realize their transgression; they have diligently and with the heart of brokenness and repentance taken it to the Lord, and they have received the Lord's instructions that this is a case that needs to be concealed.

First, it must be a case where the person who was offended knows nothing at all about the situation. If the person is aware of what you have done and you have been lying to them trying to defend yourself, it is time for you to go to them and openly repent to them and make it right.

But in the case where the offended person does not know of anything, it is sometimes better to conceal the matter. The motive for this type of concealment must be out of your love for them. It must be that you do not want to see them have to go through the emotional hurt and challenges that they will probably go through with this disclosure.

I have seen cases where revealing this type of thing destroyed a marriage and they never recovered from it. Some are so hurting that the confession of this type of trespass ends in divorce. I am not saying that it is always better to conceal this type of offense. Sometimes, it is necessary to reveal this and other types of hurting offenses to the person you have offended.

This is only one example. Before you decide to reveal everything, take it to the Lord in prayer, and be humbly and honestly open to His directions in this matter.

Note: If the issue is an ongoing stronghold or struggle, it needs to be exposed and revealed.

Chapter 7

Cut off the Access of Sin that Opens the Door to Satan

Eph 4:27 Neither give place to the devil.

The sixth principle of the seven sons of Saul is to cut off access in your life to the devil. The above scripture warns us not to give any place to the devil. In other words, do not open any doors or do things that will give Satan a pathway into your life. In Genesis 4:7 God told Cain that if he disobeys, then *sin lieth at the door*. It's like sin is crouching down waiting at the door for an entry way to get in your life.

Even though we are saved and covered by the blood of Jesus Christ, there are certain sins and demonic activities that we can get involved in that opens the door and gives access for Satan and curses. If we want to close the door to Satan and curses in our lives, we must begin closing those demonic doors. The following are several ways that we can open doors and allow Satan access and bring curses and generational curses to our lives.

Satanic Practices and Occultism

Thou shalt not make unto thee any graven image, or any likeness of any thing that is in heaven above, or that is in the earth beneath, or that is in the water under the earth: Thou shalt not bow down thyself to them, nor serve them: for I the LORD thy God am a jealous God, visiting the iniquity of the fathers upon the children unto the third and fourth generation of them that hate me. Ex 20:4-5

In the above passage God's Word tells us that He visits the iniquity upon (judges and punishes) those who hate Him. The devil hates God. He hates everything about and from God. He hates God's people, God's Word, God's praises, and anything that has anything to do with God. The devil will never be able to change or repent of his hateful spirit and nature of God or anything connected to God.

Because of his hatred for God, his perverted and evil spirit, and his warring against God and the people of God, he is his eternally cursed, and hell shall be his eternal cursed place. Unless a person is demonized, no one in their right mind would say that they hate God. However, our actions and things we affiliate with play as much of a role in determining our love or hatred of God as what we say from our mouths.

The greatest cause of curses and generational curses in people's lives, families, and generations are occultism and satanic practices. These evil and demonic practices open the door and connect us to Satan and demonic spirits like nothing else. These things bring us into direct contact with evil spirits, and thereby open us up to receive the curses in our lives and the judgment of God upon us. This happens whether or not we do them intentionally or unintentionally, knowingly or unknowingly. The following are a list of some of them:

- Involvement in witchcraft, satanic practices, and occultism
- Seeking to foretell the future by means of psychics, fortune tellers, diviners, astrology, or by any other means other than the Spirit of God.
- Participating in séances or any attempt to contact the dead
- Watching demonic occult movies
- Involvement in demonic games
- Sexual perversions and abominations, such as homosexuality, lesbianism, pedophilia, bestiality and incest
- Pornography, voyeurism, and other sexual sins of the eyes and mind
- Constant use of certain profane (curse) words—self-induced curses
- Continual defiance and disobedience to God and His Word
- Blatant refusal to repent and receive Christ, while being open to evil spirits.

In the scripture passage we used earlier, it says that God sends generational curses upon them that hate Him. Again, to engage in any satanic practice (intentionally or unintentionally) makes you an enemy against God because you are connecting yourself and your spirit with the spirit of the one (Satan) who is a hater of God. As a result, you open yourself up to curses and generational curses.

In the scripture passage we used earlier, it says that God sends generational curses upon them that hate Him. Again, to engage in any satanic practice (intentionally or unintentionally) makes you an enemy against God because you are connecting yourself and your spirit with the spirit of the one (Satan) who is a hater of God. As a result, you open yourself up to curses and generational curses.

It's the military's equivalence of trading sides and joining the side of the enemy, putting on their uniform, and fighting for and with them. This is actually what happens spiritually when a person engages in these types of activities.

A person's involvement in satanic activities places Satan's spirit upon them. So instead of having the spirit of Christ upon them that brings upon them God's mercy, forgiveness, favor, and blessings, instead, they are besieged with the spirit of Satan that brings upon them God's judgment, curses, and wrath.

B. Continual, Blatant Disobedience

What shall we say then? Shall we continue in sin,
that grace may abound? God forbid...
(Rom 6:1-2)

In the above passage Paul asks a rhetorical question. Then he answers it with an emphatic "No." We can't expect to continue to walk in rebellious sin and expect God's grace to continue to cover us. Whenever we sin against God and walk in continual, blatant disobedience to God and His Word, we inadvertently open the door for the judgment and penalty of sin to be assessed and applied to our lives. Even though Jesus died on the cross to pay the eternal price for our sins and curses, we can still open the door through continual unrepentant sin for Satan's reentry.

I emphasize continual, blatant disobedience because I believe that it's not necessarily the one sin (although in some cases it could be), but rather, the path of continually and rebelliously committing sin that opens the door for the devil in our lives.

Go and Sin No More

There are two occasions in the New Testament where Jesus told someone to *"go and sin no more."* The first instance is when Jesus healed a man *(John 5:1–15)*. Later on, Jesus saw the man and told him to stop sinning or a worse thing would come upon him. Jesus knew what had caused the man's infirmity. The specifics of the man's cause were not revealed in the Bible, but the context shows that it was caused by sinful deeds. Jesus was warning the man that if he continued and returned to the same path of sin that devastating things could come upon his life.

The second occasion where Jesus said this to someone is the story of the woman taken in the act of adultery *(John 8:3–11)*. In this case, the woman's specific sin is revealed. By telling them both to stop sinning (go and sin no more), Jesus was warning them that continuing to sin and rebel against God and His Word could lead to devastating circumstances.

The more we continue to sin and rebel against God and walk in blatant disobedience, the more we give Satan access to come upon or against us. Also, the more we sin and disobey God, the more we open the door to give access for curses and generational curses to gain access to us.

Again, our eternal salvation has been bought and secured through the blood of Jesus Christ. But through our rebellious and sinful ways, we can open the door for curses and devastating things in this lifetime.

C. Failing and Refusing to Repent

Another way that we can also cut off access to Satan and generational curses is through living a repented life. Living a life of repentance is simply to repent daily (and as the Holy Spirit leads) of your sins and transgressions.

The Lord's Prayer is not a prayer that is meant to be prayed verbatim. It is an outline of principles of prayer that we should pray about each day. One of the principals of prayer that we should pray for each day is forgiveness (*"forgive us our debts..."*). We should ask for God's forgiveness for known and unknown sins each and every day. As we do this each day, it cuts off the access and closes the door to Satan's attempt to establish and maintain spiritual contact to our spirit and in our lives.

In Psalm 39:23-24 David asked God to search him, his heart, and even his thoughts. He also asked the Lord to reveal and expose any evil or wickedness in his heart to him. David asked for God to do all this so that he could repent and get his heart right with God. This is something we all should do every night before we go to sleep. As we pray the kind of prayer that David did, and repent with a truthful, sincere heart, it renews our relationship with God and cuts off any demonic access or spirits to our lives.

For the person who continues in sin and does not repent, the enemy gains more and more access to their life. It's like the devil is slowly building a bridge or portal in order to gain a steady access flow to their life and spirit. But when you begin to live a repented life by sincerely asking God to search your heart each day and repenting of things He shows you, it's like you blow up that bridge and close that portal. This cuts off access of the devil to your life and prevents him from gaining a stronghold in your life.

Chapter 8

Appropriate the Blood of Jesus Christ to Your Life

He did all the Work.
All we have to do is the Application.

Jesus Christ has done all the work for us. He left His throne in glory and came to earth to show us the way. He lived a perfect life in order that He may represent us as the perfect sacrificial Lamb of God. He was brutally beaten in order to pay the price of sin for us. He shed His blood so that His blood could eternally cover our sins before God— leaving us sinless in the eyes of God. He alone did all the work. This is why He alone deserves all the glory, the honor, and the praise. So the question is this: *"What's left for us to do?"* The only thing Christ has left for us to do is to appropriate or apply His blood to our lives.

And ye shall take a bunch of hyssop, and dip it in the blood that is in the bason, and strike the lintel and the two side posts with the blood that is in the bason... (Exodus 12:22)

In the above passage, God gave the Israelites instructions to take the blood of the Passover Lamb (representing Jesus Christ), put it into a basin, and apply it to the lintel and doorposts (representing the cross) of each home, the night before they left Egypt.

Think about it. God was the one who heard their cry. God was the one who sent Moses to deliver them. God was the one who performed all the miracles, signs and wonders, and God was the one who broke the resistance of Pharaoh and delivered and set them free. The only thing they had to do to leave Egypt alive was to take this basin of lamb's blood and apply it to their doorposts and lintel.

If the blood of the lamb was given to a home in a basin and it was not applied to the lintel and doorposts, they would not have been covered and protected from the death angel. It's the same with us. Jesus Christ has done all the work for us. The previous six things we have mentioned puts us in a position of obedience, and therefore in a place of receiving God's favor and blessings. But this seventh thing is what we do to apply the deliverance and cleansing power of the blood of Jesus Christ to our lives.

Using the Hyssop

Notice in the above passage how God instructs them to apply the blood. He told them to apply the blood of the lamb with the hyssop branch. Hyssop represents many things, but the thing hyssop represents in this passage is our mouths. The Israelites applied the blood of the lamb with the hyssop plant. We apply the Blood of the Lamb (Jesus Christ) to our lives through the hyssop of our mouths.

We were made in the image of God. The image of God is not in the form of flesh and blood, arms, legs, and so on. It is His image as a speaking spirit. God did not form the earth with His hands, He spoke it into existence. When God made man, He breathed into man the breath of life. When God breathed the breath of life into man, He was breathing the life of God into man. So part of being made in His image is being made as a speaking spirit.

Because we are a speaking spirit, we are to apply the blood of Jesus Christ to our lives with our mouths (the spiritual hyssop) the same way the Israelites applied the blood of the lamb to their doorposts and lintel.

Whatever you Bind shall be Bound

And I will give unto thee the keys of the kingdom of heaven: and whatsoever thou shalt bind on earth shall be bound in heaven: and whatsoever thou shalt loose on earth shall be loosed in heaven. (Mat 16:19)

This passage goes along with the point that we have to apply the blood of Jesus Christ with our hyssop in order to be covered from curses and generational curses. Again, some people say that since we are covered by the blood of Jesus Christ that we do not have to worry about curses and generational curses.

Again, Jesus did the work of providing the power, authority of His Name and the covering of His shed blood. But we must apply His blood with our hyssop through His name. For example: Jesus suffered and died for our sickness and diseases just as He died to redeem and release us from every curse. But, when we get sick, do we just assume we are covered by His blood and do nothing? Of course not! We break out our healing scriptures and confessions and begin the warfare of decreeing and declaring God's Word.

The above passage tells us that through Christ, God has given us the keys to the Kingdom of heaven. These keys represent His principles, truths, power, and the authority of His name and His Word. But yet He tells us that we must bind and loose. This is the same as applying the blood with your hyssop. Begin to exercise the weapons of your warfare and begin to bind, loose, and rebuke the power of any curse or generational curse against your life and family by appropriating the blood of Jesus Christ with your hyssop.

Using our Hyssop for the Word of God

In addition to using our spiritual hyssop (our mouths) to apply the blood of Jesus Christ, we are also to use our hyssop to apply the Word of God. The Word of God and the blood of Jesus Christ go together. We apply the blood of Jesus Christ through the authority of His Word. As we speak His Word with authority and apply His blood, the Lord gives us victory over the enemy.

> *But what saith it? The word is nigh thee, even in thy mouth, and in thy heart: that is, the word of faith, which we preach; That if thou shalt confess with thy mouth the Lord Jesus, and shalt believe in thine heart that God hath raised him from the dead, thou shalt be saved. For with the heart man believeth unto righteousness; and with the mouth confession is made unto salvation. (Rom 10:8-10)*

This passage helps to correlate the passage above in Exodus. They applied the power of the blood through the physical hyssop. We apply the power of the blood of Jesus Christ through our spiritual hyssop—our mouths. Again, Christ did all the work for us, but it's up to us to apply His work to our lives.

Of the many weapons that God has given us against the enemy, He has given us three weapons that the enemy cannot withstand. They are the name of Jesus Christ, the blood of Jesus Christ, the Word of God. The devil has no defense whatsoever against these weapons. But also notice that we apply each of these weapons with our mouths.

Each time we pray in the name of Jesus Christ we are using our weapons. Each time we plead the blood of Jesus Christ against the enemy and his evil works we are using our weapons. And, each time we decree and confess God's Word against our circumstances we are using our weapons.

2 Cor 10:4-6 declares that the Weapons of our Warfare are mighty. They *pull down the devil's strongholds, cast down imaginations, and every high thing that exalts itself against the knowledge of God...* We must know that our weapons are real and that they are mighty and powerful. We must also have faith in the powerful, unstoppable force of our weapons.

When you boldly apply the Blood to your life with your hyssop, you can also declare Isaiah 54:17 that *"no weapon that is formed against me shall prosper, and every word that is spoken against me shall fall."* Curses and generational curses are weapons in which the devil wants to use against us. But we can counteract every attempt of the devil to bring curses upon our lives when we declare with our hyssop the Blood of Jesus Christ.

* Note: The last chapter of this book is a full chapter of declarations for you to decree and declare over your life and family. I encourage you to add a few of them to your daily confessions to keep your life and family's lives protected.

Appropriating the Power through Communion

Another way that we appropriate the blood of Jesus Christ to our lives is through receiving communion. When we properly receive communion, we are also appropriating the power of the blood of Jesus Christ to our lives.

When we receive communion, we are supernaturally eating the body of Jesus Christ and drinking the blood of Jesus Christ. This is a physical act that is also a spiritual act. When we drink of the blood of Jesus Christ, the power of His blood supernaturally goes in us, through us, and into our bodies and our lives. As the power of His blood begins to saturate us, it covers our sins, removes the burdens, destroys the yokes, sets us free, and cuts off satanic access and curses to our lives.

All of this is why it is so important to receive communion in faith. It is hard to believe with the natural mind that all this happens simply by eating a piece of cracker, drinking a small cup of juice, and saying a few words. But you must understand by faith that it is not merely a cup of juice, a piece of cracker, and mere words. After you ask God to bless it, God supernaturally transforms it into the actual body and blood of Jesus Christ. It is a supernatural transformation. Through prayer, consecration, and confession, and as we eat and drink His body and His blood, we supernaturally receive His power, protection, and deliverance.

Then Jesus said unto them, Verily, verily, I say unto you, Except ye eat the flesh of the Son of man, and drink his blood, ye have no life in you. (John 6:53)

Jesus said that if we **do not** eat of His body and drink of His blood, that we will not have His life in us. The contrast of this is to say that if we "**do**" eat of His body and drink of His blood that we "**will**" have His life in us. This word **"life"** is the same word, "salvation," which is where we get the word "sozo." This word "sozo" in the Greek is health, wholeness, healing, and preservation.

By eating of His body, drinking of His blood, and applying them to our bodies and lives, we get good health, wholeness, healing, and preservation in every area of our lives that we apply. This is because when we eat the body and drink of the blood of Jesus Christ, we are consuming Him. You see, Jesus don't just give life, He is life. He don't just give healing, He is healing. He don't just give blessings, He is blessings. He don't just give protection and preservation, He is protection and preservation. And as we continually consume Him, He becomes saturated in our bodies, lives, situations, and circumstances. And, because Jesus Christ is life, consuming Him automatically counteracts any curse or generational curse against your life.

You don't have to wait until your church takes communion to have communion, you can have communion in your home anytime you desire. When you have communion, use your hyssop to release the power and deliverance of the blood and body of Jesus Christ over specific areas of your life. If you see or sense an attack of the enemy against your life in any area, partake in communion and decree and declare the power of the cross and the blood of Jesus Christ against the enemy and that attack.

Communion should be taken at least once or twice a week. In fact, many choose to receive communion each and every day. Whenever you desire to commune with God, partake in communion. Whenever there is a need or crisis in your life, take communion. Begin to appropriate the power of the blood and body of Jesus Christ to your life with your hyssop and receive the power of God and your divine release.

* Note: For more information, and step by step instructions on taking and receiving communion, see our book entitled, *"Decreeing Your Healing."*

Chapter 9

Decrees and Declarations for Curses

This chapter contains over 32 powerful, anointed, and Biblically authoritative decrees, declarations, and confessions that will cover you, your family, generation, and your bloodline from curses. This is a powerful and awesome arsenal for you to use in addition to your daily prayers and confessions. As the Lord leads, I would really encourage you to add at least four or five of these daily to your prayers and confessions.

Just as you pray and cover yourself from other attacks of the enemy in your life and family such as sickness and disease, poverty, finances, and other attacks, you must also continually cover your life and family from these curses and attacks. Remember, Christ died for all of these. But we must understand that the devil is a roaring lion seeking whom he can devour and attack. Therefore, we must also be diligent, faithful, and determined to speak God's Words of protection and defense. And, as we are faithful in properly covering ourselves from these attacks and curses, then we too can boldly declare, that no weapon formed against us can prosper, and every word (curse or attack) that is formed against us is (condemned) disarmed and disabled.

General Decrees and Declarations for Curses

In the book of Genesis, Adam's sin, rebellion to God's Word, and willful disobedience brought many curses upon Adam and mankind. But thanks be to God, our Father, who sent the last Adam, Jesus Christ, who accomplished what the first Adam failed to do. He fully followed God and completely obeyed Him in all things. He willingly sacrificed His life, endured many brutal stripes and wounds, was nailed to and suffered on the cross, and shed His innocent blood on our behalf. With His sufferings and sacrifice, He delivered and set us free, took away the curse of the law, removed every curse from our lives, paid the penalty and wages of our sins and disobediences, and redeemed us back to God. Therefore, I claim the covering of Jesus Christ for my life and the lives of my family, from every curse of sin and disobedience of Adam, my ancestors, my sins, and any other source, curse, or penalty of sin and disobedience.

In the name of Jesus Christ I now rebuke, break, and loose my life and my family's lives from any and all evil curses operating through charms, vexes, hexes, spells, omens, jinxes, psychic powers, bewitchments, witchcraft, sorcery, divination, satanism, occultism, satanic activity, or any type of satanic games or interaction. I also rebuke, break, and loose my life and my family's lives from each and every one of these spirits that have been put upon any of our lives through any person, or passed down through our family, parents, ancestors, or generational bloodlines. I command all such demonic powers, influences, and curses to leave me, my family, and my entire generation, in the name of Jesus Christ.

In the name of Jesus Christ, I confess all the sins of my life, the lives of my family, and those of my ancestors and forefathers. I confess and repent of each and every sin, transgression, and iniquity, whether they were done knowingly or unknowingly, and Father, I ask that You would cover them with the redemptive blood of Jesus Christ. And, because of the redemptive blood of Christ, I therefore break the power of every curse and every hereditary curse, demonic stronghold, and bondage, that has been passed down to me through my family line and ancestral line, and I accept and receive the forgiveness and deliverance of Jesus Christ, who has redeemed me from every penalty and curse of the law.

As Jesus cursed the fig tree at the root and it died, by the authority of the name and blood of Jesus Christ, I curse and pull up by the root all attempts, all assignments, plots, plans, designs, activities, traps, and snares of the devil to curse my life or my family's lives in any way. I apply the blood of Jesus Christ to every root cause of every curse, and I decree them all to be made null and void, canceled, and never allowed to be manifested, never come to pass, destroyed, and rendered inoperative, and of no effect, both now and henceforth. I decree all of this by the redeemed blood of The Lord, and my Lord, Jesus Christ.

Father, Your Word says that You have set before us life and death, and blessings and curses. You have instructed us to choose life so that we may live. I ask for forgiveness for each and every time in my life that I have chosen death and curses rather than life and blessings through my disobediences, sins, iniquities, transgressions, failures, and slothfulness. Father, by the grace that You have given me in Christ Jesus, I reverse the power of every curse in my life; for Jesus Christ has paid the price and redeemed me from every curse. Through Christ and His precious blood, I choose the life and blessings of Jesus Christ, and therefore I shall live in Him, through Him, and covered by Him; and as a result, I receive His life, His blessings, His goodness, His healing, His favor, and His mercy all the days of my life.

I confess that through Christ Jesus, that I have been adopted into the family of God. I have been made a joint heir with Christ, the seed of Abraham, and a beneficiary of the covenant of grace that God made to Abraham to bless him and his seed. Therefore, I receive the benefits of God's divine covenant of blessings and protection from every curse of sin and curse of the law in the name of Jesus Christ.

When Jesus Christ was nailed to the cross, all of my sins, transgressions, and disobediences were also nailed to the cross. Therefore, the penalty and curse of my sins and disobediences were also nailed to the cross, leaving me with God's great mercy and divine exchange. I, therefore, receive the great exchange of Christ. Instead of death to my situations and circumstances in life, I receive the Zoe life of God, and the Sozo salvation of God. Instead of curses, I receive the blessings of God. And, instead of God's anger and wrath, I receive God's abundant love, goodness, mercy, and His favor. And I declare that they shall follow me and my family all the days of our lives.

I confess that I have been redeemed by the blood of the Lamb, Jesus Christ. And, because Christ has redeemed me, I refuse to walk in condemnation for the mistakes, failures, and sins of my past. For the Word of God declares that there is therefore now no condemnation for those who are in Christ Jesus. And, since I am in Christ, I confess and decree that my life, heart, mind, and soul have been set free from the spirit of gilt, shame, and condemnation. The sacrifice and blood of Jesus Christ has saved me, made me holy, sanctified me, and made me to be accepted in the beloved (presence of God). My past has been erased, my sins have been washed away and removed, my slate has been wiped clean, my name has been written in the Lamb's book of life, and my eternal salvation has been sealed by God, to live with Him forever in glory, by the wonderful, glorious, precious blood of the Lamb, Jesus Christ.

Declaring the Blood of Jesus against Curses of Infirmity

I decree according to the authority of the Word of God that I have been healed, delivered, and made whole in my spirit, soul, and body from every sickness, disease, and infirmity that has been brought upon my life or body by any and every sin, iniquity or curse, by the stripes and wounds that Jesus Christ bore for me.

I confess that when Jesus was nailed to the cross, that the curse of sickness and disease was also nailed to the cross. I also confess that I am crucified with Christ. Therefore, I declare that it is unlawful for any sickness or disease to come in or upon my body, because Jesus took all of my sickness and diseases upon His own body and nailed them to the cross once and for all on my behalf.

I decree and declare that every inherited spirit of infirmity and every inherited sickness or disease from my parents, ancestors, or race, to be loosed and released from my life and the lives of my family. And, I break every curse of infirmity and sickness in my family back to ten generations on both sides of my family in the name of Jesus Christ.

I rebuke every grip, hold, and clutch of sickness and disease that has been released upon my life from any curse, or through any generational, ancestral, or family bloodline by the power of the name of Jesus Christ.

I decree every curse, spirit of infirmity, and spirit of sickness and disease that is mingled, tied into, and intertwined into my DNA or genetic code in any way, to be loosed and cut out by the authority and power of the Word of the living God. For the Word of God is quick, powerful, and sharper than any two-edged sword, piercing even to the dividing asunder of the soul and spirit and of the joints and marrow.

Father, I declare that every hindering spirit that has been set against by body to hinder my health or my healing by any sin, generational sin, or any curse in my life, to be loosed and broken, now, in the name of Jesus Christ.

Father, let my blood be transfused with the blood of Jesus Christ; and cause the sanctifying, cleansing power of the blood of Jesus Christ to saturate my body, and cleanse every molecule, cell, organ, bone, structure, and every part and system of my body from every sickness, disease, virus, or infection in the name of Jesus Christ.

I decree that every spirit and feeling of pain and discomfort be loosed from my body in the name of Jesus Christ. Sickness, disease, and pain are a curse. But I declare that Jesus took my sickness, diseases, and my pains and carried them to the cross.

I come against and cast down every evil curse and

spirit of death and premature death in the name of Jesus Christ. For Father, You have declared in Your Word that You would give me long life and satisfy me with Your salvation.

Additional Decrees and Declarations against Curses

I break every curse issued or assigned against God's good and perfect will and His divine plan for my destiny or my future. I declare that the devil shall not be able to derail or abort any of God's good things or blessings that He has in store for my life. And, I decree that all things will work together for my good because of my love for Christ, and His precious blood that He has shed for me.

King Ahasuerus gave Esther and Mordecai his permission, authority, and power to reverse the evil and demonic plot by Haman to destroy God's people. By the name, authority, and power of a much higher King, the One who is the King of all kings and the Lord of all lords—King Jesus Christ, I reverse every curse, evil plan, evil plot, and every evil work or attempt of the devil to bring killing, stealing or destruction in my life or my family's lives. I also take authority, and I reverse any and all curses and evil influence that has been assigned against me or my family, or have passed down through my generational bloodline. I do all this by the power, authority, blood, and mighty and sovereign name of the Lord, Jesus Christ.

I cut off the flow of every evil, ancestral river flowing down to my generation, my family, or my family's bloodline. I cut off their power, flow, and access into my life or the lives of my family in any way by the name of Jesus Christ.

I recover and take back every good thing and every blessing that has been taken, stolen, or robbed from my life or my family because of any deception, sin, transgression, or curse, by the authority of the name of Jesus Christ. I take them back because God has given me the power and authority to do so in His name. Through Christ, I am the violent and the victorious, and I take back by force any loss or affliction to my health, finances, prosperity, joy, peace, and any blessing that God has intended for me or my family by the power and the authority of the name of Jesus Christ.

I decree, declare and receive God's supernatural abundant grace over every area of my life and family's lives. I declare that God's grace supersedes and abounds over every sin and curse. His grace is always more than sufficient for us. His grace expands far beyond any sin or curse and engulfs every sin and curse of mankind. There is nothing that cannot be abundantly covered, removed, and completely erased by the blood of Jesus Christ. Thank God for the awesome and eternal power of the abundant grace that He has given me through the blood of Jesus Christ.

Father, I renounce all attitudes of reliance, confidence, and trust in the flesh. Forgive me for having any other gods before You. Forgive me for putting more faith and confidence in the world and systems of this world concerning healing, doctors, medicine, finances, jobs, relationships, and any other area of my life in which I have trusted in, and been more faithful to than You. Father, help me, from this day forward, to trust in You with all my heart, and not lean to or rely on my own understanding and the world's system and provisions, in the name of Jesus Christ.

I break any ungodly covenant ties that still bind me to

anyone in my present life or my past that connects me to any evil or ungodly spirit, stronghold, or addiction. I decree that I am loosed and set free from every spiritual connection, soul ties, and every evil portal of darkness that connects me to them in any way, in the name of Jesus Christ.

I break every evil connection in my life to demons, demonic spirits, and unclean spirits that were made through any unlawful sexual sins. This includes fornication, adultery, pornography, any sexual perversion, sexual immorality, sexual abomination, or any unlawful or ungodly sexual act. I break their power, connection, and contact from my life, and I decree and declare that I am completely and totally set free from them all in my spirit, soul, and body, by the authority, power, blood, and name of Jesus Christ. For the Word of God has declared that he in whom the Son has set free is free indeed.

I renounce any and all self-inflicted curses that I've spoken, pronounced, or confessed over my life—intentionally or unintentionally. I loose and break their power from my life in the name of Jesus Christ; and I decree and declare them to be inoperative and ineffective against my life, by the authority and power of the name of Jesus Christ.

Father, I renounce any and all curses that I've spoken against any other person in my life, whether knowingly or unknowingly. This includes any negative words spoken against them in lies, gossip, backbiting, bitterness, anger, belittlement, and judgment. Instead, I pray that You would reverse each and every one of these words that I've spoken against them, and I pray that You would release blessings, goodness, and divine favor upon each and every one of them in the name of Jesus Christ.

Father, I ask for forgiveness for every curse word of profanity and profane words that I have spoken over my life or the lives of others. I ask that You would cleanse those things from my heart and my life, and sanctify my heart, mind, soul, and my life from them. I also ask that in every place where I have spoken profanity over others, that You would turn them around, and release Your blessings and favor in every place that I have spoken profane and negative words, by the cleansing power of the blood of Jesus Christ.

Father, I ask for forgiveness for robbing and stealing from You by not giving and withholding my tithes and offerings at times in my life. Forgive me for the spirit of stinginess and not giving to the poor, and for not giving when You have led me and spoken to my heart to give. I also ask for forgiveness for my family and ancestors who have robbed You in tithes and offerings, whether they did it knowingly or unknowingly. I ask that You would have mercy upon my life, and every member of my family line. I ask by Your mercy and grace that You would remove and reverse the curse of Malachi 3:9, every other curse, and every hindrance from my life and family, and instead, release Your bountiful grace, favor, and blessings upon our finances, health, and lives. I ask all this by the grace that You have given to us through the precious blood of Jesus Christ.

By the blood of Jesus Christ, I now claim every spiritual blessing that my Heavenly Father has given to me in Christ Jesus. I claim those blessings in the very place of any and all curses that have been set upon, against, or inherited in my life by any sin, act, or means, by the authority, power, and name of the Lord, Jesus Christ.

Even though there are curses out there that can take advantage of those who are unprepared and uncovered, I thank my God that through the precious blood of Jesus Christ that my family and I are completely covered from any and all curses of any kind. For, what can wash away my sin? *"Nothing but the blood of Jesus."* What can make me whole again? *"Nothing but the blood of Jesus."* Oh precious is that flow, that makes my sins white as snow, no other help or covering I know, nothing but the blood of Jesus.

I confess according to the Word of the Living God that I dwell in the secret place of the Most High, Almighty God; I am wholly and completely saturated and covered by the blood of Jesus Christ, and therefore there is no weapon, no evil power, and no curse of any kind that can prosper against my life or the lives of my family in any manner or in any way, spiritual or physical. In the name of Jesus Christ, I declare it. AMEN!

Other Books By Kenneth Scott

The Weapons Of Our Warfare, Volume 1
This is a handbook of scriptural based prayers for just about every need in your life. There are prayers for your home, marriage, family and many personal issues that we face in our lives each day. If you desire to be developed in prayer, then this is a must book for you.

The Weapons Of Our Warfare, Volume 2
It is a sequel of Volume I, and brings the prayer warrior into the ministry of intercession. It has prayers for your church, pastor, city, our nation, and many other national issues in which we should pray for. If you desire to be developed as an intercessor, then this book is for you.

The Weapons Of Our Warfare, Volume 3
(Confessing God's Word Over Your Life)
There is a difference between prayer and confession. This book gives the believer understanding about confessions and what they do in your life. It also contains daily confessions for major areas of your life. If you have Volumes 1 & 2, then you also need Volume 3.

The Weapons Of Our Warfare Volumes 1 ,2 & 3 on CD
Meditate on the Word of God as it is prayed on audio CDs. These CDs contain prayers from Volumes 1 2, & 3 (sold separately). As you hear these prayers prayed, you can stand in the spirit of agreement and apply them in the spirit to your life, situations and circumstances as you ride in your car, or as you sit in your home.

The Weapons Of Our Warfare, Volume 4
(Prayers for Teens and Young Adults)
Teenagers have different needs than adults. This is a prayer handbook that keeps the same fervency and fire as Volumes 1 & 2, but also addresses the needs of teens. This book is a "must" for your teens.

The Weapons Of Our Warfare, Volume 5, "The Warfare of Worship"
Through the warfare of "praise and worship," this book teaches you how to go on the assault against the forces of darkness and tear Satan's kingdom down in your life and circumstances. Psalm 68:1 tells us that when God arises, the enemy becomes scattered. When you praise, you raise! In other words, when you praise and Worship God, He begins to rise up on you, in you, in your presence, your surroundings, and even in your situations and circumstances. Since the enemy cannot stand God's presence, he has to scatter and flee, releasing and leaving your stuff behind.

The Weapons of our Warfare, Vol 6, "Decreeing Your Healing"
This book contains 160 spiritual warfare healing declarations that will help you decree and declare your healing. It also contains vital principles and precepts that will help you to understand that you have a blood bought right (by Christ) to be healed. Get this book and learn how to "take by force" your healing through the authority of God's Word.

Praying in Your Divine Authority

Many Christians are hindered and defeated by Satan simply because they do not know the dominion and authority they have in Christ. This book teaches the believer how to bind and loose Satan and demon spirits, and how to pray and walk in our divine authority.

The Witchcraft of Profanity

When people use profanity, they think they are simply speaking empty, vain words. These words are not vain at all. They are actually witchcraft spells, evoking demon spirits upon their life and the lives of those they speak over. Get this book for yourself and for others, and learn what's actually going on in the spiritual realm when profanity is used. Once you read this book, you will never use profanity again!

When All Hell Breaks Loose

Most mature Christians can survive a casual trial here and there, but many of God's people fall during the storms of life. Get this book and learn how to prevail through the storm *"When all Hell Breaks Loose."*

The Warfare of Fasting

Jesus said that some spiritual strongholds, hindrances and bondages will only be broken through prayer and fasting. This book teaches the believer the different types of fasts, the methods of fasting, and the warfare of what happens in the spiritual realm when we fast. If you want to see "total" deliverance in your life, you need to get this book.

Standing In The Gap

In this book Pastor Scott teaches life-changing principles of what it means to make up the hedge, stand in the gap, stand in agreement, and intercede for others. If you are a prayer warrior, an intercessor, or you have a desire to be one, this book is a "must" for you.

The Basics of Prayer — Understanding The Lord's Prayer

Just about all of us have prayed "The Lord's Prayer," and even know The Lord's Prayer by memory. But very few of us really understand the depths of what Jesus was truly teaching His disciples in this prayer outline. This book gives the believer a scripture by scripture breakdown of this prayer and gives illumination and insight on its understanding.

Why We Act Like That!

Pastor Scott traces the root cause of many African American issues of today to the spirit of slavery. He parallels the problems the Children of Israel had with post Egyptian bondage to issues African Americans now face in the post slavery era. He shows us that it's a slavery mindset that is still influencing many of the issues that African Americans deal with to this very day. He also shows us how we can overcome them through the power of God, His Word, and deliverance

Order at: prayerwarfare.com.

Contact Us:

For questions or comments, write to:

Spiritual Warfare Ministries
Attention: Kenneth Scott
P.O. Box 2024
Birmingham, Alabama 35201-2024

(205) 853-9509

Website:
www.prayerwarfare.com
or
spiritualwarfare.cc

Email us at — prayerbooks@aol.com

This book is not available in all bookstores. To order additional copies of this book, please order on our website above. If you would like to mail your order, send $10.99 plus $2.98 shipping and handling to the above address.

36261511R00062

Made in the USA
Middletown, DE
16 February 2019